"In another life, Nelson Wolff would have made a great sportswriter.
The Elysian Fields of Baseball is a must read for those wanting to dive into a book penned by an author with a deep love for the game and skilled at straightforward, insightful commentary."

—Tom Osborn, Sportswriter
San Antonio Express-News

THE ELYSIAN FIELDS

of

BASEBALL

THE SPIRITUAL EVOLUTION
OF AMERICA'S GAME

NELSON W. WOLFF

ISBN: 978-1-958407-30-1 (Hardback)

ISBN: 978-1-958407-31-8 (Soft Cover)

Cover image via Wikimedia Commons: *The American National Game of Base Ball. Grand match for the Championship at the Elysian Fields, Hoboken, N.J.*
This work is in the public domain in the United States because it was published (or registered with the U.S. Copyright Office) before January 1, 1930.

Book design by designpanache

ELM GROVE PUBLISHING
San Antonio, Texas, USA
www.elmgrovepublishing.com

Elm Grove Publishing is a legally registered trade name of Panache Communication Arts, Inc.

CONTENTS

Dedicated to the memory of my dad, Nelson Gus Wolff, who taught me the game of life on the Elysian Fields of Baseball.

I want to thank Burl Yarborough, David Lesch, Skip Bradley and Jade Heep for reading my original drafts, and for their contributions to this book.

My wife Tracy and my dad.

1. A CELESTIAL HAVEN

THE 315-MILE HUDSON River flows from Henderson Lake, located in the Adirondack Mountains of upstate New York. It travels south to New York Harbor, winding its way between New York City and Jersey City.

For approximately 20,000 years, Native Americans inhabited the riverbanks, relying on the trees, plants, and waters for food and nourishment. Nature was their world, and they revered, glorified, and worshiped it.

When the Dutch arrived, they began exploring the river, naming it after Henry Hudson, who navigated its waters in 1609.

In 1783, Colonel John Stevens acquired a large tract of wooded land near the river in Hoboken, New Jersey. Later, he expanded his holdings by purchasing an additional 25 acres, giving him one mile of riverfront property.

Colonel Stevens and his family resided in a villa on this estate, overlooking the Hudson River. The villa was surrounded by the wonders of nature, including vegetable gardens, fruit trees, flowing shrubs, coffee plants, and exotic flora.

Believing that his picturesque rural setting, with its delightful shade and clean air, would attract those seeking refuge from the dust, smells, and noise of New York City, Colonel Stevens decided to develop the land as a public park in 1824. He named it Elysian Fields, drawing inspiration from the Greek promised land where righteous souls could dwell forever.

The Greek Elysian Fields is described as a celestial, heavenly place blessed with ocean breezes, rich soil, natural fruits, golden flowers, and splendid trees. It was believed to be located on earth, at the western edge, near the stream of Okeanos, known as the Isles of the Blessed.

Homer's *Odyssey* portrays it as a paradise where life is easiest for men, filled with fertile soil, abundant fruits, golden flowers, and magnificent trees.

Poet Hesiod described it as a realm where happy heroes relish honey-sweet fruit that flourishes twice a year.
Poet Pindar depicted it as a place ablaze with golden flowers, some blooming from trees.

The Stevens family transformed their land into a magical haven, famously known as the "Elysian Fields of Hoboken." The refreshing breeze from the Hudson River mirrored the waters of Okeanos in the Greek Elysian Fields.

It seems the Stevens family had a deep appreciation for the gods of ancient Greece. In 1830, they constructed a Grecian-style pavilion adorned with Doric pillars, dedicated to the worship of Bacchus, the god of wine, revelry, and ecstasy.

Two years later, in 1832, the Stevens family excavated a cave and decorated it with a Gothic-style stone arch. They believed that spring water from the well possessed healing powers, naming it after the Greek-Roman prophetesses known as Sibyls.

In homage to Aphrodite, the goddess of love, they created winding paths among the trees, affectionately dubbed "lover's paths."

This enchanting haven of trees, flowers, and grass— along with Sybil's cave, Bacchus's pavilion draped in grapevines, and Aphrodite's romantic paths—provided nourishment for the souls of many visitors, including notable figures like Charles Dickens, Edgar Allan Poe, and Washington Irving.

Each day, as many as 29,000 New Yorkers crossed the river by ferry to reach the Elysian Fields. An article in the New York Commercial lauded the riverside walk as the finest in the world and argued that the grounds should forever remain untouched in their rural charm.

Most important to our story is that since the 1830s, countless ballplayers from New York flocked to the park to engage in a game played on its lush green lawns, a game tracing its roots back to the stick-and-ball games of early colonists.

These games had various forms, such as town ball, barn ball, and sting ball, each governed by its own set of rules. One notable rule allowed players to tag out a base-runner by throwing the ball at him; if the ball hit him, he was deemed out.

On September 23, 1845, Alexander Cartwright and his baseball colleagues William Wheaton and William Tucker established the Knickerbocker Base Ball Club in New York. Tucker held the positions of secretary and treasurer, while Cartwright served as vice president and a member of the rules committee. They attracted players from diverse professions, including merchants, Wall Street brokers, salesmen, and physicians, all eager to take to the field and play baseball.

After examining various rules from other clubs, Cartwright and his associates crafted 20 rules, which they meticulously documented. These became known as the "Original Rules of Baseball," or the "Knickerbocker Rules," and were subsequently published and adopted by other baseball clubs.

The established rules defined "fair" and "foul" territory, permitted three strikes for batters, limited each inning to three outs, and replaced the rule allowing runners to be hit by the ball with the requirement for tags and force outs. The playing field was designed as a diamond rather than a square, and an umpire was assigned to each game. With some modifications, many of these rules are still in use today.

In keeping with the noble traditions of entering the Greek Elysian Fields, strict personal conduct rules were put in place for players. Those who used profane or inappropriate language were fined 25 cents for each offense. Additional fines were levied if a player questioned an umpire's decision or disobeyed a team captain.

Several New York ball clubs, including the Knickerbockers, the Magnolia Ball Club, and the Gothams, traveled by ferry from lower Manhattan to the Elysian Fields. Approximately 50 New York ball clubs participated in play there, and as baseball's popularity grew, the number of clubs increased to around 130. The official written record of an American baseball game was created on June 19, 1846, when the Knickerbocker Baseball Club faced the New York Nine at the Elysian Fields in Hoboken. The Knickerbockers lost the game to the New York Nine, with a final score of 23-1.

The Knickerbockers maintained a scorecard of that game, which still exists today. Their record-keeping practices laid the groundwork for baseball's tradition of tracking more individual player statistics than any other sport.

Wheaton recognized the significance of the Elysian Fields for baseball, stating, "Those fields were truly Elysian to us in those days. There was a broad, firm greensward, fringed with fine shady trees, where we could recline during intervals, waiting for a strike (a turn at bat) and taking a refreshing rest."

Frank Pidgeon, a store clerk who played for the Eckford Baseball Club, reflected, "We had some merry times among ourselves. We would forget our business and everything else, on Tuesday afternoons, go out into the green fields, don our ball suits, and go at it with a perfect rush. At such times we were boys again. Such sports as these brighten a man up and improve him both in mind and body."

Daniel "Doc" Adams, who became president of the Knickerbockers in 1846, reminisced, "Once we were free from all restraint and, throwing our coats off, we played until it was too dark to see. Sometimes we had as many as a hundred spectators watching us."

After a regularly scheduled game, aspiring players took to the field to learn the game, giving rise to what became known as a "muffin" game. Q.K. Philander Doesticks humorously chronicled one such game in the *Hartford Courant*:

> *"I squared myself, raised my big stick, and told the Pitchman to pitch in. He did so. The first ball came like a cannon shot, but I dodged it neatly. The next one hit me plump in the breast. I dropped my stick and asked him what he did that for."*

When Doesticks finally made contact with the ball, he collided with the catch man, tumbled over the umpire, and ultimately crashed into the fence. His antics earned him the title of "The dashiest muffin who ever held a club." It was an enjoyable occasion for all involved.

The ballplayers shared a grand time playing America's game on the Elysian Fields. The ballfields forged a magical connection between baseball and the beauty of nature. The mystique, lore, legends, and traditions of baseball thrived on the vibrant energy of the Elysian Fields, creating a unique spirituality that intertwined the sport with the natural world.

Three years after the official introduction of the Knickerbocker game, Cartwright moved to the West Coast in 1849 and later to Honolulu, where he became the city's first fire chief. He also served as King Kalakaua's financial advisor.

Cartwright is credited with bringing baseball to Hawaii. He wrote a letter to Charles DeBost, stating that he possessed:

> *"...the original ball with which we used to play on Murray Hill."*

"Many is the pleasant chase I have had,'" he fondly recalled.

His sons, Bruce and Alex, played baseball in Honolulu during the 1860s.

Cartwright passed away on July 12, 1892, and is buried at Oahu Cemetery, previously known as Makiki Park, where baseball was once played. His large pink granite monument is visited by many ballplayers, including Babe Ruth in 1934.

On August 26, 1939, "National Cartwright Day" was celebrated at Ebbets Field in Brooklyn, where a pineapple juice toast was made in his honor. And now, I raise a toast to him as well.

Cartwright was inducted into the Hall of Fame in 1938. While Wheaton, Tucker, or Doc Adams could have also been recognized as the father of baseball, historians seemingly drew straws and chose Cartwright.

During my last visit to the Hall this past summer, I sought out the plaque commemorating him. Few would notice it, as it is a small plaque among the over 200 Hall of Fame members. The plaque features a picture and bears the inscription "Father of Modern Baseball."

In 1857, the Knickerbockers and 15 other teams founded the National Association of Baseball. The Association adopted three key features that still endure today: ninety feet between the bases, a nine-man team, and a nine-inning game. Just nine years after the founding of the amateur baseball association in 1857, the organization had grown to encompass 100 teams.

Consider how different the game would be if the bases were only four feet closer together. This change would end exciting double plays. Conversely, if the bases were four feet farther apart, we would see more double plays and fewer hits. What a brilliant decision that was!

Henry Chadwick (1824-1908) was a cricket player, and cricket is one of the sports that influenced the development of baseball. In the 1850s, Chadwick played cricket on the Elysian Fields and attended several baseball games.

After watching a match between the Eagles and Gotham clubs, he noted, "It was not long before I was struck with the idea that baseball was just the game for America." Over the next 50 years, he dedicated himself to writing about it.

In 1859, he published a box score of a game in the *Clipper* newspaper. This idea took hold, and box scores from various teams spread across the country. From these box scores, statistical measurements for players were developed, allowing a player today to measure themselves against those who played 100 years ago.

From the very beginning, amateurs were adamant that players should not receive payment for playing. They viewed money as a corrupting influence in a game meant to set a shining example for youth and fans alike.

For over 50 years, baseball was played on the Elysian Fields of Hoboken. Some refer to this site as the birthplace of modern baseball, while others argue that its inception occurred in New York. Regardless, it is undeniably the "cradle of baseball," where young men played for the love of the game amid the splendor of nature.

The games took place on open fields without fences,

echoing the lyrics of Robert Fletcher, who wrote, "Don't fence me in; give me lots of land and breeze and cottonwood trees."

However, the idyllic landscape of Hoboken was soon to change as economic development progressed along the Hudson River, leading to the construction of warehouses and piers that encroached upon the Elysian Fields.

In the 1890s, articles began to appear, signaling the end of the Elysian Fields. Many had headlines such as "Time's Destroying Touches," "Historical Retreats," and "Landmarks of Early Days Being Rapidly Obliterated."

The hallowed grounds were transformed into a modern street grade, culminating in the construction of a Maxwell House coffee plant in 1939. Only a plaque remains to mark the location of the former ball fields, representing a tragic failure of elected officials to safeguard both nature and the cradle of baseball.

While nature gave birth to the American game of baseball in the enchanting Elysian Fields of Hoboken, today the game is played on thousands of elysian fields—both those without fences and those surrounded by fences and grandstands.

From the transcendental essence of Hoboken's Elysian Fields, baseball emerged as a timeless game, played at a pace and rhythm reminiscent of a ballad's meter. The fluid movements of the players resemble those of a ballet; an infielder glides toward the ball, scoops it up, and makes a seamless throw to first base, all in one graceful motion. There is a natural cadence to the game as it progresses.

Beginning as a pastoral pastime, baseball evolved into a blend of intellectual engagement and rural charm, played with pride and camaraderie in the serene embrace of nature, without the constraints of a clock. Its beautiful pace and rhythm are unmatched by any other sport.

*   *   *

In 1999, I attended the Society for American Baseball Research (SABR) conference in Phoenix, Arizona. Founded in 1971, the organization, which boasts over 6,000 members, promotes the study of baseball as a vital American social and athletic institution.

Approximately 400 attendees participated in a variety of seminars and presentations. These ranged from John Rayburn's demonstration of baseball radio re-creations to Dave Cain's insights on "Baseball South of the Border," Eddie Gold's exploration of baseball songs and poems, and Sky Andrecheck's ranking of baseball dynasties.

The most intriguing baseball story I heard was shared in the hallway by John Husman. As we talked between sessions, he recounted the story of his team, the Great Black Swamp Frogs Base Ball Club from Sylvania, Ohio.

He explained, "We play a version of baseball that hearkens back to the game's origins. Our team travels across the country, demonstrating to fans how the game was once played by the Knickerbockers.

We adhere to the same rules utilized by the Knickerbockers. While the batter gets three strikes, foul balls do not count against them. We use wooden bats that are not tapered, and the pitcher throws underhand from a distance of 45 feet.

Like the Knickerbockers, we refer to our team as the 'home nine,' the batters as 'strikers,' the catcher as the 'behind,' and runs as 'aces.' We also follow the standards of conduct established by Cartwright in the 1840s."

I asked, "What was the ball like?"

He responded, "In the early years, balls were handmade, with many variations. Efforts in the 1850s aimed to standardize baseballs, which were set to weigh between 5.5 and 6 ounces and have a circumference of 8 to 11 inches.

Our ball features a rubber core and is tool-stitched, with one side lacking stitches. It is not tightly wound. They are slightly smaller and more expensive, costing about $35 each."

I then inquired, "What about the uniforms?"

He replied, "We wear special uniforms modeled after those first worn by the Knickerbockers in 1851, the first recorded team to adopt uniforms. Like them, we don long blue woolen trousers, white flannel shirts, and straw hats. Our wives also attend the games, dressed in the styles of the 1840s and '50s."

I said, "What a great tradition you are keeping alive."

He concluded by saying, "We do not want people to forget that baseball started as a gentleman's game, played by amateurs on the Elysian Fields of nature."

While the New York ballplayers found their Elysian Field in Hoboken on the banks of the Hudson River, as a young boy I would find mine along the banks of the San Antonio River.

The father of baseball, Alexander Cartwright.

2. THE PASTORAL FIELDS
OF MY YOUTH

DAD WOULD TAKE MY brothers George, Gary, and me fishing and swimming in the San Antonio River, which flowed south near our home, bordered by lush greenery. My brother George and I explored the riverbanks and camped out, reminiscent of Native American traditions.

In 1857, Frederick Law Olmsted, the architect of New York City's Central Park, visited San Antonio and described it as follows:

> *"The whole river gushes up in one sparkling burst from the earth. It has all the beautiful accompaniments of a smaller spring: moss, pebbles, seclusion, sparkling sunbeams, and dense, overhanging, luxuriant foliage. The effect is overpowering."*

The San Antonio River and its surroundings resembled the Elysian Fields of Hoboken. Public parks, such as Espada Park and Mission County Park that bordered the riverbanks, where visitors hiked, had picnics, and played pickup baseball games. Semiprofessional games also took place at Richter Field. The cool breezes drifting from the river provided refreshing relief.

I became captivated by the river's mystique and the

power of nature, much like the Native Americans who had camped and hunted along its banks for approximately 10,000 to 12,000 years. About 200 sub-bands of Coahuiltecan Indians fished, gathered edible plants, and camped along the San Antonio River.

Like the Native Americans living along the banks of the Hudson River they believed the natural world was intricately connected to all aspects of life. Their spirituality, rooted in nature, served as a vital force in shaping their understanding of existence.

Their prayers were deeply intertwined with the natural world. They saw themselves as part of the herbs, fir trees, morning mist, clouds, flowing waters, wilderness, dewdrops, and pollen.

One poem, attributed to various sources and appearing in several different versions since the 1930s (most often titled "Native American Prayer"), beautifully expresses this connection in the following extract:

> *And I shall swallow the Earth whole*
> *when I die.*
> *And the Earth and I will be one.*
> *Hail the Earth, my mother.*
> *I give you this one thought to keep*
> *I am with you still—I do not sleep*
> *Do not think of me as gone*
> *I am with you still—in each new dawn.*

On Sundays, our family enjoyed picnics by the riverbanks. Dad would play catch with us while we watched older boys engage in pickup baseball games. One Sunday, Dad delivered a sermon to my brothers and me, much like a preacher.

He said, "We are all born with a soul released into life alongside our bodies, holding the mystery of what makes us unique. Soon, as you grow a little older, I will teach you the game of baseball, where you will learn to unlock your soul by playing amidst the wonders of nature, just as I did. The spirituality of nature, combined with the lore and tradition of baseball, will infuse you with the energy of the universe to guide your ambitions, hopes, and dreams. This blend of spirituality and tradition is passed down through generations, carrying stories, beliefs, and customs that can profoundly shape your character.

"Baseball will also prepare you to embrace life's risks and teach you to persevere through setbacks. The game is marked by failures, punctuated by brief moments of exhilaration. Even with eight teammates on the field, you can often feel isolated. No one can assist you while you're at bat, fielding, throwing, or pitching. When you're at the plate, you'll likely fail more often than you succeed; even the best hitters achieve a hit only one out of three times. Yet, you must strive for that double, triple, or home run to offset those failures.

"Baseball underscores the importance of taking risks on the field—stealing second base, charging the plate on a squeeze bunt, and diving for a line drive in the outfield instead of waiting for it to bounce."

Dad was transferring his love of baseball to us, and we embraced it. Born in 1919, he came of age working on a 600-acre farm with his father in Pflugerville, Texas. Like many farm boys of his era, he learned the game and played pickup matches on makeshift diamonds carved out of the pastoral landscape.

When he was 13, in 1932, the Great Depression forced his parents, Adolph and Emma Wolff, to lose their farm in Pflugerville. They packed Dad and his siblings into an old Model A

and moved to San Antonio to live with relatives in a neighborhood filled with other German American families.

After completing eighth grade at Paige Junior High
School, Dad dropped out to support the family. Despite this,
he continued to play baseball, joining the Veltman Kids, a team
founded by former Major League player Arthur Patrick Veltman, who played in the majors from 1926 to 1934.

During my research for this book, I was surprised to find
a digital copy of the June 27, 1937, edition of the San Antonio Light
newspaper. It featured a photograph of Dad with a serious ex-
pression, the bill of his cap tilted slightly to the left.

The article announced that he would be starting the
first game for the Highland Park semi-professional team, established in 1937 and made up of players from Highland Park and
Denver Heights in southeast San Antonio.

In 1939, while having lunch at the Red Top Inn, Dad met
my mother, Marie Williams. Like him, she had dropped out of
school and was working as a waitress for her cousins, Billie Jo
and Myrtle Williams. Dad was quickly smitten by her beauty.
He proposed, she accepted, and they married in 1940.

I was born at 9:00 a.m. on October 27, 1940, as my
grandparents joined my mom and dad in their bedroom at 619
McKinley Street in south San Antonio. Doctor Moore charged
just $15.00 for the delivery, and I still have the receipt.

Mom scooped ice cream for Better Home Ice Cream,
while Dad stacked lumber for Campbell Lumber Company.
My grandfather Adolph worked as a janitor at the McKinley
Avenue Methodist Church, and my grandmother Emma took
in laundry. Together, they managed to stretch their earnings to
enter the fringes of the working middle class.

The house where I was born has since been torn down
and is now a vacant lot next to the freeway, which disrupted

south side neighborhoods when it was built in the 1960s.

My brother George was born on July 18, 1942. Like me, he was born at home, this time at 202 Regina Street, just a few blocks from where I was born. That house still stands today. In 1947, the last of the Wolff siblings, Gary, was born at Baptist Hospital, a fact that particularly pleased my mom.

Poet and writer Robert Bly suggests that a boy's psyche develops a hole when he lacks visibility of his father's work, filling that void with demons of suspicion.

My dad embraced the instinctive world of masculinity, earning his manhood through shared experiences with his father and friends while laboring in the corn and maize fields. He also worked part-time as a bartender alongside his father, allowing his father's customers to exchange experiences and pass down the essence of their souls.

Since I couldn't accompany my dad to work, I first entered the instinctive world of masculinity while sitting on his lap as he played poker and talked baseball with his friends. Once a week, Dad and his friends gathered in our detached garage to play poker. The garage was preferred over the house for its cooler atmosphere created by the open door. With beers, cigarettes, and cigars in hand, they played for dimes, quarters, and the occasional half dollar. For them, gambling symbolized manhood—a test of taking chances at the poker table.

It was at this poker table that I was first introduced to baseball, a sport that dominated America's cultural landscape in the 1940s.

The players often reminisced about watching Joe DiMaggio and the Yankees in an exhibition game against the San Antonio Missions minor league club in 1941, where DiMaggio impressively went 5 for 5.

They debated whether DiMaggio's 56-game hitting

streak surpassed Ted Williams's batting average of .406 in 1941. Most agreed that Williams's achievement held more significance since he chose to play in the last doubleheader instead of sitting out, which could have left him with a 399.5 average, effectively considered as .400. Instead, he played and went 6 for 8, achieving the .406 average.

Their discussions also included Ross Youngs, regarded as the best major league player from San Antonio. Youngs played for the New York Giants from 1917 to 1926 and went 2 for 5 against the San Antonio Missions during spring training on March 30, 1918. With a lifetime batting average of .322, he contributed to the Giants' World Series championships in 1921 and 1922.

Dad recalled that Youngs was a favorite of manager John McGraw, who displayed only a picture of Christy Mathewson and Youngs in his office. Tragically, Youngs's life was cut short by Bright's disease at age 30. He was inducted into the National Baseball Hall of Fame in 1972 and the San Antonio Sports Hall of Fame in 1998.

After Dad's lecture on the banks of the river about the merits of baseball and with the stories I heard at the poker table, my brother George and I began playing when we lived on Astor Street. I was ten years old, and George was nine. Across the street was Kite Field, a large open area where everyone flew kites. It also had a ball field with a backstop, a rough infield, and no outfield fences.

On summer days, George and I would wake up, open the blinds, and peer across Astor Street to Kite Field, eager to see if our baseball friends had arrived. We would grab our bat, gloves, and a baseball, rushing across the street within minutes to join them for a pickup game. Our little brother Gary, just three years old, would chase after us to watch us play.

On Saturday and Sunday mornings, Dad would come

over to play catch and throw batting practice, teaching us the fundamentals of the game.

When we weren't on the field, we listened to the radio with Dad to catch Yankee games. Mel Allen was the voice of the Yankees during the golden age of radio broadcasting before television became dominant.

Listening to the radio in the 1940s, I could almost visualize the amazing grace of "Joltin' Joe" DiMaggio, known as "the Yankee Clipper," as he glided across the green grass of center field, making incredible catches and showcasing his powerful swing as he hit home runs.

DiMaggio played for 13 seasons, and when he retired in 1951, he was asked why he decided to step away. He replied that he could no longer live up to the name DiMaggio.

He was selected for the All-Star team each year and was inducted into the Hall of Fame after his retirement.

His marriage to film star Marilyn Monroe only added to his mystique, inspiring songwriters and authors to create works about him. Paul Simon's lyrics, "Where have you gone, Joe DiMaggio? Our nation turns its lonely eyes to you," helped to immortalize him.

Later, when DiMaggio met Simon, he supposedly remarked, "What do you mean? I haven't gone anywhere."
In Ernest Hemingway's *The Old Man and the Sea*, the old Cuban fisherman expresses a desire: "I would like to take the great DiMaggio fishing."

Although the first baseball game was televised on May 17, 1939, few people owned television sets at that time. It was 1947 when the first World Series was broadcast. It wasn't until 1950 that my father was finally able to buy a television set. That year, we watched the inaugural televised All-Star Game on July 1.

Dad bought us baseball cards along with sticks of bubblegum. The practice of producing baseball cards began in the 1860s when the Peck and Snyder Sporting Goods store started making them, a tradition later adopted by tobacco companies. An 1886 cigarette card of Mike "King" Kelly gained considerable popularity.

By the time we started collecting in the 1950s, baseball cards had already surged in popularity. We amassed hundreds of cards, but somewhere along the way, we lost them. Some of those cards, including a Mickey Mantle card, would become very valuable.

In an August 2022 auction by Heritage Auctions, Mantle's Topps 1952 mint-condition card sold for $12.6 million to an anonymous buyer. The seller, Anthony Giordano, had purchased the card in 1991 for $50,000.

Dad introduced us to military baseball, which has a long history dating back to the Civil War. The most famous player to participate in military baseball in San Antonio was Dizzy Dean, who played for the Fort Sam Houston army team. His 16-year-old brother, Paul, worked at a filing station on St. Mary's Street while also pitching for the Pierce Tire and Bicycle Shop team.

After leaving the army in 1929, Dizzy began working for the Public Service Utility Company in San Antonio and pitched for the CPS team. Just six months later, he reported for spring training with the St. Louis Cardinals.

In 1934, he achieved remarkable success by winning 30 games, while his brother Paul, known as Daffy, won 19 games for the "Gashouse Gang" Cardinals, leading them to a World Series victory.

From 1932 to 1936, Dizzy led the league twice in wins, shutouts, and four times in strikeouts. He was inducted into the Hall of Fame in 1953.

By the 1940s, all five major military bases in San Antonio had baseball teams. The military league comprised the Kelly Field Fliers, Fort Sam Houston Rangers, Randolph Field Ramblers, Brooks Field Ganders, and San Antonio Aviation Cadet Center Warhawks.

Additionally, two military teams located near San Antonio also participated in the league: the San Marcos Navigators and the Hondo Comets.

We had the opportunity to watch Enos Slaughter play military ball. During his 19-year career in Major League Baseball he was a ten-time All-Star. Slaughter was later inducted into the National Baseball Hall of Fame and passed away in August 2000.

In 1953, the Chicago White Sox played at Fort Sam Houston's Christy Mathewson Field. Minnie Minoso, who debuted in the major leagues in 1948—just one year after Jackie Robinson broke the color barrier—hit an inside-the-park home run at Mathewson Field. He would eventually be inducted into the Baseball Hall of Fame.

I remember one night while running along the stands at a military game when I fell and hit my chin, with my tongue caught between my teeth. My mother quickly rushed me to the emergency room, where they stitched me up. It was my first baseball-related injury.

In 1947, when I was six years old, dad took us to see the Double-A Missions play in their new stadium, a 9,500-seat venue at the intersection of Mission Road and Mitchell. Across Mission Road was Richter Field, which extended down to the San Antonio River, while Mission Conception, one of the four Spanish missions, stood across Mitchell Street.

I still vividly recall the excitement of attending my first game at Mission Stadium, which was regarded as one of the finest minor league ballparks in the country, attracting fans from far and wide.

My brothers and I were proud members of the Knot Hole Gang, granting us free admission to the games. We had a special spot in the bleachers where all the kids would gather, cheering for the Missions while enjoying a simple feast of Cracker Jack, soda, and hot dogs as we watched the game unfold.

The Missions compete in the Texas League, founded in 1888 with six teams. They played their first game at Muth's Park on Government Hill, near Fort Sam Houston.

In 1897, an exhibition game was played under temporary lights at a time when electricity was not yet widespread. Over 1,000 spectators attended San Antonio's first night game, but it would be another 30 years before another game was held under the lights.

Like many regional minor leagues, the Texas League experienced instability. San Antonio withdrew from the league in 1889 and 1890, and there was no league play at all in 1891. However, play resumed in 1892, and our team relocated from Muth's Park to San Pedro Park.

After the 1899 season, the league suspended operations for two years, and San Antonio did not have a team until 1903.

In 1906, our team moved to Electric Park, and in 1913, we relocated to League Park. Then, in 1932, we moved to Tech Field at San Pedro Park, leading up to the new ballpark we attended in 1947.

The 1949 season stands out in my memory, particularly because the Brooklyn Dodgers played an exhibition game against the Missions. I watched as Jackie Robinson, who had broken the color barrier in 1947, hit 3 for 5, helping the Dodgers secure an 8-1 victory over the Missions. The game drew a crowd of over 8,000 fans, including 3,000 African Americans who were seated in the segregated "Jim Crow" section.

Six years after Robinson's groundbreaking achievement, the San Antonio Missions introduced their first two African American players: Harry Wilson and Charlie White. Unfortunately, discrimination continued to limit their dining and accommodation options.

In 1951, the Yankees visited, featuring their exciting new 18-year-old star, Mickey Mantle, alongside the legendary Joe DiMaggio. The game on April 5 attracted more than 11,000 fans. DiMaggio shone, going 2 for 3, while rookie Mantle managed just one hit in six at-bats.

Watching both Mantle and DiMaggio was thrilling, but we also had our eyes on 20-year-old Bob Turley. That season, he won 20 games, struck out 200 batters, and made headlines by striking out an astonishing 22 batters in a remarkable 16-inning game. He subsequently advanced to the major leagues, won the Cy Young Award, earned three All-Star selections, and pitched in two World Series with the Yankees.

While enjoying military and minor league games, listening to baseball on the radio, and playing at Kite Field, we were on the brink of a lifetime baseball experience. In 1952 my dad, as the terminal manager for Texas Consolidated Transportation Company, persuaded the company to sponsor a semi-pro baseball team. The Transporters became one of over 1,000 semi-pro teams nationwide.

Dad got George and me jobs as batboys for the Transporters, even buying us uniforms adorned with TCTC letters across the front. Our outfits consisted of knee-length pants, baseball socks, tennis shoes, and TCTC caps. A photograph of us in those uniforms was published in the June 1952 issue of Tanker Talk, the company's monthly magazine.

Every summer weekend, we donned our uniforms and

rode with Dad and Mom to the west side of town. Van Daele Stadium, built in 1923, was situated on land owned by the Herman Van Daele family. Van Daele had arrived in San Antonio in 1893 as one of several Belgian vegetable farmers who settled in the area, passing away in the same year the stadium was constructed in his honor.

The Transporters played in a semi-pro league at Van Daele Stadium, competing against teams like the North Side Mustangs, South Flores Auto Sales, and Zepeda Drive-In. Under the guidance of Captain Blas Monaco, a former major league player, TCTC won the championship.

Dad envisioned a dedicated baseball field for the Transporters and directed my cousin, Lloyd Schwartz, the team manager, to negotiate a lease for Richter Field. The ballfield was owned by Richter Bakery.

Founded by William Louis Richter in 1882, the bakery started in a single room, producing and delivering fresh bread and cakes. It later expanded to a larger facility and reached a production level of 110,000 loaves per day. In addition to running the bakery, Richter served as an Alderman and became Mayor Pro Tempore after the death of Mayor Callaghan in 1912. Richter passed away in 1940, the year of my birth and the year Richter Field was built. The family operated the bakery for 100 years before dissolving the business in 1997.

Richter Field was located along the banks of the San Antonio River, surrounded by large trees and grassy areas, just off Mitchell Street. It extends down to Mission Road, directly across from Mission Stadium.

In January 1953, my dad authorized Schwartz to negotiate a five-year lease with Henry Richter, the vice president of Richter Bakery. Texas Consolidated agreed to paint the stands and fences, build a concession stand, restrooms, and a press box. Dad also committed to returning all entry fees and any surplus funds beyond operational costs to the ball teams.

The lease was signed, and work began immediately. The outfield fences needed repairs and painting, the field was in poor condition, and the stands required fixing.

My brother George and I joined the work crew to restore Richter Field. Every day after school, we walked from Riverside Elementary School on School Street to the ballpark. We took a route one block over to Roosevelt Avenue, then down to Mitchell Street, and finally to the field. Once there, we cut and watered the grass, raked the infield, picked up rocks in the outfield, and helped with painting.

As we spent time with the experienced baseball players, George and I learned invaluable lessons. We joined them for practices, games, and post-game gatherings, where we truly absorbed the essence of baseball, with our dad and his friends right beside us.

In 1953, the Transporters boasted an outstanding team featuring former Major League players like Blas Monaco (Cleveland Indians, 1937 and 1946) and Texas Jack Kraus (Philadelphia Phillies, 1943-45; New York Yankees, 1946). Alex De La Garza had also played Triple-A ball in the Detroit Tigers organization.

During batting practice before games, George and I played in the outfield, chasing down balls and leaping over the fence to retrieve them when they sailed over. Beyond the right field fence, we could see the stands of Mission Stadium across Mission Road, where balls often flew into the street.

Beyond the left field fence, a collection of broken-down carnival rides beckoned us to explore. We often lingered there after climbing over, searching for lost balls and playing on the rides. One day a dog chased George, but George held his ground, making the dog back off. We quickly scrambled back over the fence.

During practice, the seasoned players taught us the fundamentals of the game. I learned that playing baseball required strategy; you had to think ahead. You needed to know where to throw the ball if it was hit to you and stay alert on the base paths, avoiding the mistake Babe Ruth made when he ended up at third base with two other runners in the same situation. Understanding the strengths and weaknesses of the pitcher or hitter was essential.

We were reminded to keep track of the pitch count and, most importantly, not to run off the field like Fred Merkle did on September 23, 1908. His teammate had a walk-off hit, but it didn't count because Merkle failed to touch second base before a player tagged it for a force-out.

The seasoned players offered us advice such as, "Keep your eye on the ball," "Stay loose," and "Bust your butt or get off the field." They provided plenty of guidance but offered few compliments. The highest praise came when they acknowledged a good play by saying, "Hey DiMaggio, good catch!"

One time, during batting practice, I caught a high fly ball and heard Dad hollering from the stands, "Watch my boy! He's a ballplayer." He was sitting right behind the catcher, enjoying a cold beer in his concrete box seat.

During the games, the Transporters' former pros gave it their all. We watched as shortstop Alex De La Garza glided toward a grounder, flipping it to Blas Monaco, who raced to second base. Monaco then side-armed the ball to Tommy Rock, who stepped on first base for a double play.

Players slid into bases like Ty Cobb, sprinted after grounders and fly balls, argued with umpires, and heckled the opposing team. In the dugout, we observed them chewing tobacco, spitting it out, and sharing stories from their time in the "Big Show." They were earthy, tough, and fiercely competitive, filled with rich experiences from their professional baseball careers.

De La Garza carried a press clipping recounting how he struck out Mickey Mantle while pitching in relief for the Toledo Mud Hens against the Kansas City Blues. Monaco bragged about tagging out Joe DiMaggio at second base, while Big Jack Kraus boasted about the games he won as a pitcher for the Yankees. We could never get enough of those tales.

After the games, we kids rushed onto the field for pickup games until it grew too dark to see. While we played, the old pros and our parents drank beer and danced on a concrete slab, illuminated by strings of lights along the banks of the San Antonio River, just a few hundred yards from the ball field. When night fell, we would join the players, our parents, and their friends.

Nearby, a small building housed a jukebox that they often played. On certain nights, a live band entertained the crowd. George recalled a day when Dad asked him to pick pecans from the trees lining the river. When George returned, Dad declared that he hadn't picked enough. He was a tough taskmaster.

As a reward for our work as batboys, Dad arranged for several of his employees to pick up my friends, George and me, from Riverside Elementary and take us to my birthday party by the San Antonio River. Several of the old pros attended, making it the best birthday I ever had.

On weekend nights, Dad invited the Mission and Transporters to the company club on Roosevelt, just a few blocks from the stadium. Company employees and their families mingled with the players, enjoying drinks, dancing, and playing shuffleboard and poker.

A poker game occurred in a back room that was off-limits to kids and wives. When a player emerged from that room, I could see Dad sitting at the table, his black felt fedora tipped back, studying his cards while taking swigs of cold beer and sliding dollar bills into the pot. After much pleading, he would sometimes let me join, and I would stand behind him as $5, $10, and $20 bills piled high in the pot.

Most of the time, we kids played shuffleboard with the ballplayers, while the moms gathered around a table, listening to music, sometimes dancing with each other, and at other times with the players.

Being bat boys as not enough baseball for George and me. In 1953, Dad signed us up for Little League Baseball, marking the same year we became batboys for the seasoned pros.

Little League had only been around for 12 years when we began playing, having started in 1939 with a three-team league in Williamsport, Pennsylvania. The first Little League World Series took place there in 1947.

George and I played in the Laura Steele Little League at the Highland Park field on the south side, just off Rigsby Road. George played shortstop while I pitched for the McCreless Home Builders.

Dad attended our practices and closely worked with our coaches, Ed Swindle and Morris Renfroe, to help us prepare for our games. Dad told me that I should focus on fastballs and changeups. If you throw curves, sinkers, and sliders, they will put excessive stress on your arm that is not fully developed.

During our games, dad would sit in the stands with Mom, often placing bets with his friends on how many batters I would strike out—a wager he usually won.

It was here that George and I officially entered the enchanting world of baseball. We learned to compete, develop our skills, and support one another as teammates. We were un-covering the secrets of our souls, just as Dad had promised.

The magical year of 1953 was particularly significant for me, as I was fully inducted into the instinctive realm of baseball alongside my dad and his friends. Dad and the old pros of Texas Consolidated prepared me for life's challenges.

All my childhood baseball heroes have since passed on to the Elysian Fields, where they will eternally play the game they love.

Sadly, Richter Field has been destroyed, much like the mythical Elysian Fields of Hoboken. It was purchased by CPS Energy and transformed into an industrial site. Mission Stadium was demolished to make way for the Bexar Juvenile Courts and a juvenile detention center. The Laura Steele Little League fields and Kite Field have also disappeared. The wonders of our base-ball youth have faded, leaving only cherished memories.

As I write this book, 71 years after that enchanting year of 1953, the names of the old Transporters remain vivid in my mind and heart: catcher Dick Cody, first baseman Tommy Rock, second baseman Blas Monaco, third baseman Manuel Chicon, shortstop Alex De La Garza, right fielder Joe Naranjo, center fielder Boots Gaubatz, left fielder Dick Hood, and pitcher Jack Strauss. The manager was my cousin, Lloyd Schwartz.

In the fall of 1953, I entered the 7th grade at Page Middle School, just as my dad had in 1932. I played football for Page and boxed at the Boys Club across W. Drexel Street from the school. Before spring arrived in 1954, my dad announced that he had been transferred to Houston to manage the largest truck termi-nal that Texas Consolidated owned. The thought of leaving San Antonio filled me with dread.

When we arrived in Houston that summer, my brother George and I joined a teenage summer league. In the fall, I entered Pershing Middle School, where I met my closest friend, Glynn Dyess. Together, we played football for Pershing and baseball during the summer.

In the fall of 1956, I started my freshman year at Bellaire High School, ushering in a carefree experience filled with football, baseball, chasing girls, and learning through osmosis. We dressed in rolled-up jeans, loafers, white t-shirts, and red jackets, trying to emulate James Dean from *Rebel Without a Cause*.

I became an officer in the Bellaire Varsity Club, which, if I may say so, was my highest academic achievement. One day, my school counselor remarked that I was performing well below my I.Q. I was pleased to hear that I had a high one. Although I wasn't excelling academically due to my refusal to study, I was still gaining valuable life lessons on the baseball field.

In the summer of 1957, George and I played for the Bellaire Cardinals in the Texas Senior Teenage League. That summer, we won the state championship, and a photo of our 1957 championship team now hangs in my home library.

During our senior year in 1959, I became the captain of the baseball team, leading us to win the city baseball championship. I also played defensive halfback on the football team, contributing to our impressive record of 9 wins and 2 losses.

Fortunately, my dad was enjoying a winning streak and told me to visit the Mercury dealership to pick out a car for George and me.

Accompanied by Glynn, I selected a striking orange 1959 Mercury featuring a powerful 290-horsepower V8 engine. The car became even more impressive after George added tailpipes on each side and hung large Styrofoam dice from the rearview mirror.

The year 1959 marked the end of my carefree youthful days playing the game I had grown to love.

In the next chapter we will take a look back to how the early evolution of amateur baseball led to the emergence of professional baseball. This will provide you with a better understanding of how the professional game of baseball changed the game that was once played on the Elysian Fields of Hoboken.

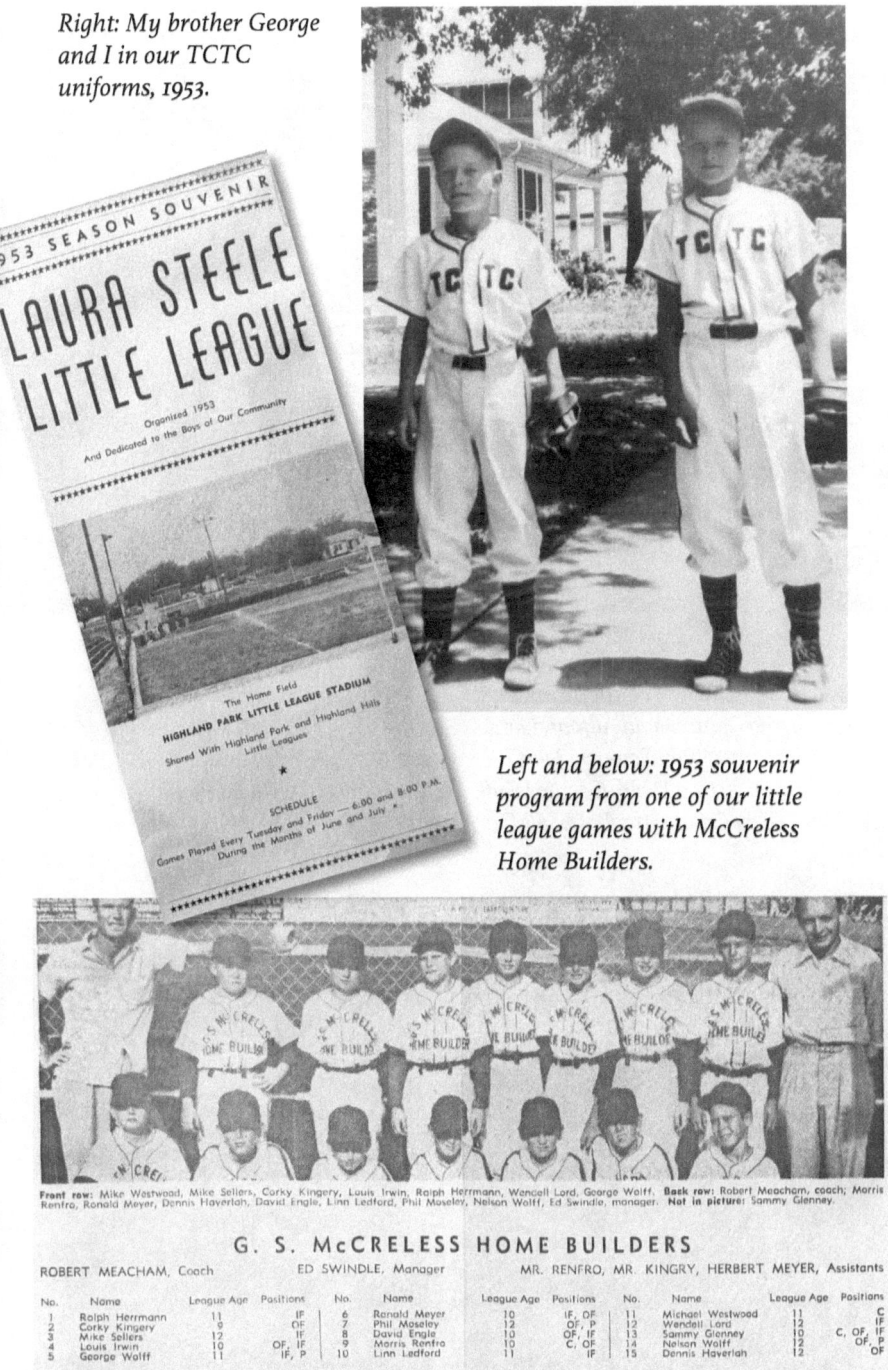

Right: My brother George and I in our TCTC uniforms, 1953.

1953 SEASON SOUVENIR

LAURA STEELE LITTLE LEAGUE

Organized 1953
And Dedicated to the Boys of Our Community

The Home Field
HIGHLAND PARK LITTLE LEAGUE STADIUM
Shared With Highland Park and Highland Hills
Little Leagues

★

SCHEDULE
Games Played Every Tuesday and Friday — 6:00 and 8:00 P.M.
During the Months of June and July

Left and below: 1953 souvenir program from one of our little league games with McCreless Home Builders.

Front row: Mike Westwood, Mike Sellers, Corky Kingery, Louis Irwin, Ralph Herrmann, Wendell Lord, George Wolff. Back row: Robert Meacham, coach; Morris Renfro, Ronald Meyer, Dennis Haverlah, David Engle, Linn Ledford, Phil Moseley, Nelson Wolff, Ed Swindle, manager. Not in picture: Sammy Glenney.

G. S. McCRELESS HOME BUILDERS

ROBERT MEACHAM, Coach   ED SWINDLE, Manager   MR. RENFRO, MR. KINGRY, HERBERT MEYER, Assistants

No.	Name	League Age	Positions	No.	Name	League Age	Positions	No.	Name	League Age	Positions
1	Ralph Herrmann	11	IF	6	Ronald Meyer	10	IF, OF	11	Michael Westwood	11	C
2	Corky Kingery	9	OF	7	Phil Moseley	12	OF, P	12	Wendell Lord	12	IF
3	Mike Sellers	12	IF	8	David Engle	12	OF, IF	13	Sammy Glenney	10	C, OF, IF
4	Louis Irwin	10	OF, IF	9	Morris Renfro	10	C, OF	14	Nelson Wolff	12	OF, P
5	George Wolff	11	IF, P	10	Linn Ledford	11	IF	15	Dennis Haverlah	12	OF

Above: Richter Field, where the semi-pro TCTC played.

Below: George and I on the Texas Senior Teenage champion team, 1957. Back row, left to right: David Allums, Gordon Scarborough, Winston Herman, Norman Jones, Tom Pennick, John Rice, Manager Maury Howard.
Front row: Nelson Wolff, George Wolff, Dennis Mabry, David Redford, John Crain, Gary Calabretta. Bat boy Mike Allums.

3. THE RISE OF THE OLIGARCHS

THE TRADITION OF AMATEUR baseball on the Elysian Fields of Hoboken continued through the Civil War. In 1860, during Abraham Lincoln's presidential campaign, a lithograph depicted him playing baseball against his rival. The image featured Lincoln holding a bat and ball, hitting a home run while his opponents struggled with much weaker bats.

After Lincoln became president, he and his son Tad watched games played behind the White House. Lincoln even participated in children's games, sprinting between bases with his long legs and flapping coattails.

During his presidency, the Civil War fueled interest in baseball throughout the South. Both Union and Confederate troops played the game in the winter and early spring when military activity slowed.

Baseball also thrived in prison camps, where it was played almost daily. Otto Boetticher, a Union soldier, painted a scene of Union soldiers playing at Salisbury Prison in North Carolina.

Following the Civil War, baseball's popularity soared. In 1867, the Knickerbockers hosted the first Ladies' Day game.

By that year, the National Association of Baseball Players included 300 clubs. They upheld the principle of keeping baseball an amateur game, just as it had been on the Elysian Fields of Hoboken, and were committed to maintaining unpaid players, believing that money would corrupt the sport.

Though they sought to protect the game from financial influence, they inadvertently paved the way for professional baseball as fan attendance at their games increased. In 1865, stands were constructed for spectators, and shortly after, fences were erected to ensure that only paying customers could view the games. As a result, the baseball boys lost their access to open fields and cotton wood trees.

Baseball, once cherished by amateurs for the love of the sport, underwent a significant transformation when former Knickerbocker player Harry Wright began charging admission to games in 1858. By 1860, some players were receiving compensation for their participation.

In 1869, Wright established the Cincinnati Red Stockings, the first professional baseball team. Serving as both manager and center fielder, he offered his players salaries seven times higher than the average working man's earnings, with the highest-paid player earning $1,400 per season.

The Red Stockings quickly became Cincinnati's pride, winning every game in their first two seasons. However, financial troubles forced the team to disband after just two years.

Wright was later inducted into the Hall of Fame in 1953.

In 1871, the same year the Red Stockings disbanded, a rift emerged within the National Association of Baseball Players. Some members sought to maintain baseball as a gentleman's game, while others pushed for professionalization. This divide culminated in a walkout by the amateur faction during the association's annual meeting, resulting in the formation of the National Association of Professional Base Ball Players. This split significantly contributed to the decline of the amateur National Association.

The new professional league soon struggled to achieve competitive balance and financial stability among its teams, causing initial efforts by affluent owners to commercialize the sport to falter.

However, two savvy businessmen arose, demonstrating how to successfully transform professional baseball into a profitable venture.

William Hulbert, a prominent businessman, became the president and majority owner of the Chicago White Stockings. In 1876, he enlisted pitcher Albert Spalding from the Boston Red Stockings. Spalding was recognized as the premier pitcher of his time, boasting an impressive win-loss record of 252-65.

By the age of 27, in 1878, he was appointed president of the White Stockings and later became a part owner of the team. With Spalding's support, Hulbert established the National League of Professional Base Ball Clubs in 1876, now simply known as the National League. This new league introduced a full schedule of games, banned alcohol and gambling at events, and prohibited games on Sundays.

Additionally, the league adopted the reserve clause, which bound players to the teams with which they signed contracts. While this provided stability for team owners, it restricted players' ability to pursue better-paying contracts, effectively relegating them to the status of indentured servants. The league also unjustly excluded black players from participation.

As president of the White Stockings, Spalding created a team that dominated the 1880s, winning five pennants and even managing the team for one year. The White Stockings eventually became known as the Chicago Cubs.

At the same time, Spalding and his brother opened a sporting goods store, which expanded to 14 locations. They also ventured into the manufacturing and distribution of sports equipment, including baseballs and the first commercial gloves and bats.

Spalding successfully lobbied the league to adopt the baseballs manufactured by his company, effectively ending the use of homemade balls that varied in size and weight.

In 1886, he became the first team owner to introduce spring training, hosting the inaugural session in Hot Springs, Arkansas. This innovation quickly gained popularity among other teams, leading Hot Springs to be recognized as the birthplace of spring training.

From 1888 to 1889, Spalding organized the first global tour featuring major league players. The team played in Honolulu, Hawaii, where Cartwright resided at the time. However, there are no records indicating that Cartwright met Spalding or attended any games, suggesting he may not have been present, particularly since he believed baseball should remain an amateur sport.

In 1908, Spalding authored *America's National Game* and produced several books under the title "Spalding Athletic Library."

Fourteen years after his death, he was inducted into the National Baseball Hall of Fame in 1939. Hulbert received the same honor in 1995.

The successes of Spalding and Hulbert were partly attributed to Mike "King" Kelly, the most colorful and accomplished player of his era. He spent most of his career (1878-1893) with the Chicago White Sox and the Boston Beaneaters. Kelly was a two-time National League batting champion, a three-time National League scoring leader, and a six-time National League champion.

A true innovator on the basepaths, Kelly developed the hook slide and the fadeaway slide. He popularized the hit-and-run play and was the first catcher to back up throws to first base.

Kelly earned the nickname "$10,000 Beauty" when the owner of the White Sox sold him to the Boston Beaneaters in 1886 for the highest price ever paid for a player. When Kelly initially resisted the sale, Spalding warned, "I will make him eat hay with his horses." Kelly was transferred to Boston.

Once in Boston, he became widely known as "King" Kelly. During the offseason of 1892-1893, he performed on the vaudeville circuit at the Imperial Music Hall in New York, starring in the play *King Kelly, the Monarch of the Baseball Field.* Kelly wrote an autobiography titled *Play Ball*, becoming the first player to do so. He also popularized autographing and inspired the song *Slide, Kelly, Slide.*

Additionally, he served as the inspiration for the poem *Casey at Bat*, penned by Ernest Thayer in 1888. Here is an excerpt from the poem:

> *The outlook wasn't brilliant for the*
> *Mudville Nine that day.*
> *The score stood at four to two, with just*
> *one inning left to play...*
> *A sickly silence fell upon the patrons...*
> *If only Casey could get a hit...*
> *Then there was Jimmy safe at second, and*
> *Flynn hugging third...*
> *From five thousand throats and*
> *more, a lusty yell arose,*
> *For mighty Casey was advancing to bat.*
> *The umpire called "strike two"*
> *The air shattered with the*
> *force of Casey's swing...*
> *But there is no joy in Mudville;*
> *Mighty Casey has struck out.*

Hard living and heavy drinking took their toll, and he succumbed to a deadly flu virus at the tender age of 36. Approximately 7,000 people attended his funeral. Kelly was inducted into the Hall of Fame in 1945.

In the 1880s, professional baseball was dominated by working-class players from various ethnic backgrounds, including Germans, who comprised one-third of the player population.

Many players competed without gloves or batting helmets and were treated like slaves on the plantations of their owners. Their obligations to the owners remained even without a contract.

The game was intensely competitive, with players willing to do whatever it took to win. Conflicts arose not only between players but also with umpires. Despite this, fans were captivated by the game's intensity, which had evolved into a form that would have appalled the amateur gentlemen players of the Elysian Fields of Hoboken.

Compounding the rough nature of the sport was the challenging era of urbanization in the 1880s. The expansion of cities brought crime, unsanitary conditions, and impoverished individuals living in cramped quarters. Players endured oppressive heat and subsisted on inexpensive food.

One of my favorite books on early professional baseball is Edward Achorn's *Fifty-Nine in '84*, which tells the stories of some of the toughest players from the late 1880s. Among them was "Old Hoss" Charlie Radbourn, who began his major league career in 1880 with the Buffalo Bisons, a National League team. Radbourn was a sullen, hard-drinking workhorse who pitched nearly every day despite excruciating pain from an overworked arm. He had to adapt to pitching rule changes enacted in 1883, allowing pitchers to throw overhand instead of sidearm from below the waist.

Following this rule change, he achieved an astounding 59 wins in 1884, a single season record likely never to be broken. Over 12 seasons, Radbourn amassed a record of 310 wins and 194 losses, with an ERA of 2.68. He was later inducted into the Hall of Fame.

By the late 1890s, the game was governed by rules very similar to those we recognize today.

The greatest pitcher to emerge in the late 1890s was Cy Young. He began his career with the Cleveland Spiders of the National League in 1890 and concluded it with the Cleveland Naps and Boston Rustlers in 1911. A powerful pitcher, he accumulated 511 wins and pitched 7,356 innings—both still MLB records. He was inducted into the Hall of Fame in 1937 and passed away in 1955 at the age of 88.

While the National League of Professional Base Ball Clubs was well-organized, several other professional leagues struggled to survive. The American Association was established in 1882 and lasted until 1891. The Union League played for just one season in 1884, while the Players' League endured for only a year in 1890.

The American League, which evolved from the minor Western League, was founded in 1901 and became the only other league to endure and compete with the National League. The Federal League attempted to challenge both the National and American Leagues but lasted only two years, from 1914 to 1915.

Overall, six leagues were recognized as part of Major League Baseball, but only two have endured.

At the turn of the 20th century, both the National and American Leagues consisted of eight teams. The fierce competition for top talent and intense rivalries defined the first two decades of this era, creating an exciting period in baseball that attracted more fans to ballparks to witness the emergence of new stars. This time is referred to as the Dead Ball Era.

Photo via Wikimedia Commons

Founder of the National League, William Ambrose Hulbert.

4. THE DEAD BALL ERA

THE DEAD BALL ERA encompasses the first two decades of the 20th century, during which rubber-core baseballs limited both the distance and speed of play. The game emphasized a strategy known as "small ball," focusing on bunts, singles, stolen bases, and hit-and-run plays.

Success during this time required players to exhibit exceptional speed, agility, glove work, and situational awareness, both offensively and defensively. Athletes with greater agility tended to excel in this style of play, showcasing skills distinct from those required in modern baseball that features power hitters.

In October 1903, the first World Series was held, with the American League's Boston Red Sox defeating the National League's Pittsburgh Pirates. This event would eventually become one of the most beloved sporting events in the country.

During this period, Major League Baseball (MLB) was working to establish a more structured framework, creating the National Baseball Commission, which included the presidents of each league and a permanent chairman.

By 1909, average attendance at Major League games had tripled since 1901, reaching approximately 9,000 fans per game. This surge attracted the attention of President William Howard Taft, who in 1910 became the first president to throw a ceremonial first pitch at the start of a season, tossing the ball to the renowned pitcher Walter Johnson in the nation's capital. This tradition continued annually until President Kennedy's time and has persisted, with some interruptions, ever since.

Despite facing challenges during the Dead Ball Era—including competition from the Federal League for two years, inadequate ballparks, and the influence of gambling—this period also produced outstanding players who would become some of the game's greatest legends.

One of the most dominant figures of this era was "The Georgia Peach," better known as Ty Cobb. His fame rivaled that of Mike "King" Kelly, who had dominated the game in its early days.

I own a 1961 first edition copy of *My Life in Baseball: The True Record*, written by Ty Cobb with help from journalist Al Stump. General Douglas MacArthur wrote an introduction stating, "Few men have left a finer imprint upon the history of our time than that of Ty Cobb."

Thirty-three years later, Al Stump changed his stance and published *Cobb: The Life and Times of the Meanest Man Who Ever Played Baseball*. Released in 1994, the book was a controversial work by a journalist notorious for fabricating stories and who had been banned from multiple newspapers and magazines due to his dishonesty and false reporting.

But Ty Cobb was a tough player, a characteristic of many players during the Dead Ball Era. He was known for his aggressive demeanor, fierce nature, and sometimes uncontrollable temper. Fans appreciated such players and often enjoyed the arguments and fights that accompanied the game.

Cobb came from a prominent family; his father, Herschel, was a state senator. Although he loved his father deeply, his life was shattered in 1905 when his mother accidentally killed him, mistaking him for an intruder. Throughout his playing career, Cobb carried the burden of wanting to excel for his father, a heavy weight he ultimately overcame.

He married and raised five children over 39 years, and they described him as tender and loving. Cobb also advocated for the inclusion of African Americans in professional baseball.

Cobb spent most of his career during the Dead Ball Era, from 1905 to 1919, before transitioning to the Live Ball Era in 1920, where he continued to excel until his retirement in 1928.

Throughout his career, Cobb set 90 MLB records and achieved remarkable statistics, including 4,065 runs scored and an impressive lifetime batting average of .366. Inducted into the Hall of Fame in 1936, Cobb was ranked third on *Sporting News'* list of "Baseball's 100 Greatest Players" in 1999.

Another notable player from that era, often viewed through a controversial lens due to the 1919 Black Sox scandal, was Shoeless Joe Jackson. Unlike Cobb, Jackson grew up in poverty. His difficult upbringing began at age seven when he was forced to work 12-hour shifts in textile mills to help support his family. As a teenager, Jackson was recruited by mill owners to play baseball for the mill's team, earning $2.50 per game.

He never learned to read, remaining illiterate throughout his life.

Despite this challenging start, he emerged as one of the best natural hitters in history. In 1911, during his first full MLB season with the Cleveland Naps, Jackson achieved an astounding .408 batting average, a record that still stands for rookies. He was traded to the Chicago White Sox in 1915, where he played until 1920.

His career was brief, lasting only 12 years and ending at the age of 32 due to the 1919 Black Sox scandal. Jackson's lifetime batting average of .326 ranks as the fourth highest in MLB history.

In 1999, he was ranked 35th on *Sporting News'* list of the 100 greatest players, and fans voted him the 12th greatest outfielder of all time. He was also a finalist for MLB's All-Century Team but has not been inducted into the Hall of Fame.

An intriguing connection exists between Shoeless Joe Jackson and Ty Cobb. In the late 1940s, Cobb visited Jackson at his liquor store in Greenville, South Carolina, three decades after Jackson was banned from baseball at the age of 32.

When Jackson failed to acknowledge him, Cobb remarked, "I know you. You're Joe Jackson. You can't pretend with me."

Jackson replied, "I wasn't sure you wanted to know me. A lot of those guys back then just don't."

Cobb wanted Jackson to sign a baseball for him. Jackson asked him to return the next day, but Cobb said he was just passing through and suggested they might do it another time. Unfortunately, they never saw each other again.

During the Dead Ball Era, pitchers were considered the kings of baseball. They benefited from rubber-core baseballs that were rarely replaced during games, allowing them to throw spitballs and scuffed balls.

This era boasted legendary pitchers like Christy Mathewson, Grover Cleveland Alexander, Cy Young, and Walter Johnson. Had Babe Ruth continued to pitch, he might have joined their ranks. He pitched from 1914 to 1919, winning 96 games for the Boston Red Sox and contributed to three World Series victories.

Emerging from the cornfields of Kansas, Walter Johnson ranks among the greatest pitchers of all time. Born in 1887 on a rural farm just four miles from Humboldt, Kansas, he was one of six children. At 14, he and his family moved to California, where he played high school baseball before relocating to

Idaho to play in the Idaho State League.

In 1907, he was signed by the Washington Senators, where he spent his entire career until 1927. Johnson became known as a power pitcher, renowned for his sidearm delivery.

In Johnson's rookie year, Ty Cobb and his teammates heckled him during their first game against him, shouting, "Get the pitchfork ready, Joe; your hayseed is on his way back to the barn!"

When Johnson faced Cobb, he threw a pitch that Cobb later described as hissing with danger. Cobb remarked that nobody could touch Johnson's powerful arm, which he regarded as the most formidable he had ever encountered.

Throughout his career, Johnson recorded 3,508 strikeouts, a record that stood for 50 years. Although this record was eventually surpassed during the Live Ball Era, Johnson's feat is particularly noteworthy given the rarity of strikeouts during the Dead Ball Era. No other pitcher exceeded 1,000 strikeouts, except for Cy Young, who played most of his career in the 1890s.

Johnson played his entire career with the Washington Senators from 1907 to 1927. Despite being part of a losing team, he achieved 417 wins, the second-most in baseball history. Remarkably, he lost 65 games due to his team's failure to score.

He recorded 110 shutouts, the most in history, and won the Triple Crown three times, excelling in ERA, wins, and strikeouts. He was named Most Valuable Player twice.

After retiring as a player, Johnson managed the Senators from 1929 to 1932 and the Cleveland Indians from 1933 to 1935, finishing with a managerial record of 529 wins and 432 losses.

He was one of the first five players inducted into the Hall of Fame, collectively known as the "Five Immortals." Additionally, he is a member of both the MLB All-Century Team and the MLB All-Time Team.

Johnson passed away at the age of 81 on December 6, 1955.

Emerging from the coal mines of Pennsylvania, Honus Wagner became known during the dead-ball ear as one of the greatest position players and power hitters in baseball history. Born in Carnegie, Pennsylvania, he was one of nine children. He dropped out of school at age 12 to help his father in the coal mines and began playing sandlot baseball with his brothers.

He played for the Louisville Colonels for three years starting in 1897. He then played 17 years for the Pittsburgh Pirates from 1900 to 1917. It didn't take long for "The Flying Dutchman" to be recognized for his unusually strong physique, well-suited for baseball. Standing 5 feet 11 inches tall, weighing 200 pounds, and possessing a barrel chest, massive shoulders, long arms, and large hands, he appeared shorter due to his bowed legs.

A five-tool player, Wagner excelled in throwing, fielding, hitting for average and power, and displayed speed on the base paths.

He finished his career with a lifetime batting average of .328, accumulating 3,420 hits, 101 home runs, and 1,733 RBIs. Wagner was an 8-time NL batting champion, a 4-time RBI leader, and a 5-time stolen base leader.

What is particularly extraordinary about his accomplishments is that he achieved them during the Dead Ball Era, a period dominated by pitchers.

He appeared in two World Series: the first in 1903, which the Pirates lost, and the second in 1909, when they emerged victorious.

Historian and statistician Bill James regards Wagner as the greatest shortstop of all time, crediting him with the greatest single season of any player in history. In 1908, he posted a remarkable .354 batting average with 109 RBIs, competing against pitchers with an ERA that was half of what it is today.

Had Wagner played in the Live Ball Era, which favored hitters, his numbers would likely have soared.

Wagner is a member of both MLB's All-Century Team and All-Time Team. James ranks him second, behind Babe Ruth, and he was one of the first five inductees into the Hall of Fame.

His T206 baseball card sold for $6.6 million, making it the second most expensive sports card in history.

The end of the Dead Ball Era arrived with a disheartening chapter: the 1919 Black Sox scandal. The White Sox, the strongest team in baseball that year, were heavy favorites to defeat the Cincinnati Reds in the World Series.

However, with money from gambler Arnold Rothstein, eight White Sox players—including Shoeless Joe Jackson—were bribed to throw the Series.

After the regular season, 29-game winner Eddie Cicotte delivered a lackluster performance in the opening game, igniting rumors of a fix. In the second game, Lefty Williams, who was nearly as skilled as Cicotte, also faltered and lost.

Dickey Kerr, the third pitcher, was unaware of his teammates' involvement in the scandal and managed to win two games during the Series.

Though Eddie Cicotte redeemed himself by winning the third game he pitched, this victory was merely for appearances, as the Reds ultimately clinched the series five games to three.

Even before the 1919 Black Sox scandal, gambling had been a longstanding issue in baseball, tainting the sport due to the pursuit of money. The warnings from the amateur players of Hoboken's Elysian Fields were proving to be accurate.

To protect the integrity of professional baseball, Major League Baseball was compelled to take action. Savvy baseball fans recognized that the three-man commission of team owners was ineffective in addressing the gambling problem.

In 1920, National League President John Heydler emphasized the necessity for a commissioner with the authority to enforce rules. In November of that year, the stern Judge Kenesaw Mountain Landis was appointed as baseball's first independent commissioner.

At that time, Landis was serving as a U.S. District Court Judge for the Northern District of Illinois, having been appointed by President Theodore Roosevelt in 1905, where he served for 17 years.

The Judge encountered no criticism from lawyers and upheld strict decorum in his courtroom. He was unafraid to confront large corporations. For the first two years of his tenure as Baseball Commissioner, he continued to perform his duties as a District Court Judge.

Just two months before his appointment, a grand jury had been convened to investigate allegations of game-fixing, particularly surrounding the controversy involving the White Sox series.

On August 2, 1921, a jury found the players not guilty of accepting bribes, despite four White Sox players confessing to throwing the World Series in exchange for payment. Unfortunately, these written confessions were lost.

The following day, Commissioner Landis announced, "Regardless of the verdicts of juries, no player that throws a ball game, or promises to throw a game, or associates with crooked players and gamblers where games are planned and fails to inform his club will ever play professional baseball again."

He subsequently banned eight White Sox players from professional baseball for life, taking decisive action against the influence of gambling in the sport. Over his career he banned 18 players, thus restoring integrity, respect, and credibility to Major League Baseball.

One of the banned players was Shoeless Joe Jackson. Although Jackson may have accepted a bribe to throw the World Series, he did not perform poorly; he recorded 12 hits in the series, a record that stood until 1964. He also led both teams with a .375 batting average, committed no errors, and even threw out a runner at the plate.

In 1999, the U.S. House of Representatives passed a resolution urging MLB to lift Jackson's ineligibility, but to this day, the league has refused.

The scandal, along with the transition to the Live Ball Era, caused some fans to turn their backs on baseball, most notably sportswriter, columnist, and author Ring Lardner, a member of the MLB Hall of Fame. Lardner wrote for the *Chicago Examiner* and the *Tribune* and was a devoted fan of the Chicago White Sox.

Following the scandal, Lardner expressed his disgust with the game's moral decline. In 1921, he stated that the emergence of Babe Ruth and power hitters had turned him away from the sport.

A prime example of Lardner's writing can be found in his book *You Know Me Al*. It features fictional letters from bush leaguer Jack Keefe to his friend, filled with humorous lines such as, "Although he is a very poor fielder, he is a very poor hitter."

After addressing baseball's gambling issues, Commissioner Landis laid the groundwork for Major League Baseball to become a powerful organization, solidifying its monopoly that over sports did not have and establishing an oligarchy without peers.

In 1915, the Federal League filed a lawsuit against the National League, claiming a violation of the Sherman Antitrust Act. Landis played a crucial role in delaying the case, ultimately contributing to the Federal League's collapse and the resulting establishment of an MLB monopoly.

In 1922, during Landis's second year as commissioner, the Supreme Court ruled that Major League Baseball was exempt from the Sherman Antitrust Act. Justice Oliver Wendell Holmes wrote the majority opinion, asserting that professional baseball represented a form of recreation and entertainment. This ruling has consistently withstood subsequent challenges.

This decision was notable as it does not extend to the NFL, NBA, or NHL, thereby granting MLB team owners substantial power.

During Landis's 24-year tenure as commissioner, he mandated that minor leagues be affiliated with the major league draft. He required all major league teams to disclose their transactions with minor league teams and prohibited them from concealing prospects, ensuring a clear pathway for players to reach the MLB.

Two weeks after his death in 1944, he was elected to the Hall of Fame.

When the Dead Ball Era ended in 1920, baseball entered the Live Ball Era, which continues to this day. One team and one player led the way: Babe Ruth and the New York Yankees.

"Shoeless" Joe Jackson.

5. THE YANKEE DYNASTY

IN 2000, I JOINED 100 devoted Yankee fans for the chance to meet and play ball with stars from the Yankee dynasty. All participants were men aged 40 to 75, each contributing $4,500 to spend five days at Tampa Bay Stadium, a replica of Yankee Stadium.

My motivation for attending was my involvement in senior league hardball and my work on a book titled *Baseball for Real Men.*

As I entered the stadium in Tampa, Florida, I felt a rush of excitement at playing in a venue reminiscent of the 1923 "House That Ruth Built." The stadium boasted a green frieze façade along the front of the triple-deck grandstand, much like its New York counterpart. This copper façade had developed a distinctive green patina over the years.

Although our smaller venue couldn't seat 58,000 fans like the original Yankee Stadium—the most iconic venue in the United States—the historical significance was still palpable. During the first game on April 18, 1923, an astounding 74,000 fans packed the stands to witness Babe Ruth hit a three-run home run. A few years later, in 2009, the owners would demolish Yankee Stadium. A terrible decision, tearing down another historic ballpark.

On our first night, we watched a video celebrating the era of Ruth and Gehrig, featuring clips of Gehrig's famous speech delivered on July 4, 1939, during a Yankee celebration. In that moment, he declared, "I am the luckiest man on the face of the earth."

This poignant speech came after Gehrig retired at age 36 due to a diagnosis of amyotrophic lateral sclerosis, then a virtually fatal condition. He passed away two years later at the age of 38.

As we sat absorbed in the moment, the background lyrics of "In my heart, I am forever young" and "These are the days you will remember" resonated deeply with our baseball-loving hearts.

Later, I struck up a conversation with a fellow camper, Gus Gussack, Chairman of the General Bearing Corporation, who had grown up in New York.

"Did you ever see Ruth play?" I asked.

Gus replied, "I attended Babe's last game at Yankee Stadium in 1934. Along with the other kids, I yelled for Ruth to be put in the game. Eventually, the manager let him pinch-hit, and he hit the ball off the right-field wall."

I recalled, "He retired from baseball five years before my birth, but my dad saw Babe hit a towering home run over the center-field fence at League Park in San Antonio in 1930. After the game, Dad joined other kids at Municipal Auditorium, where Babe delivered a speech. That night, Ruth stayed at the historic Menger Hotel, and his picture from that time still hangs in the lobby."

Gus continued, "I was at Yankee Stadium when he spoke in May of 1948, celebrating the 25th anniversary of the stadium. A few months later, I returned to see his open casket displayed in the Rotunda, where thousands of fans came to pay their respects. I also attended his funeral at St. Patrick's Cathedral in New York. If you watch a newsreel from that time, you might spot me among the 75,000 fans gathered outside the cathedral."

While Gus witnessed the end of the Ruth era, it would have been even more thrilling to experience the remarkable beginning of the Live Ball Era in 1920 when Ruth ignited the excitement. In his first year with the Yankees, he hit 54 home runs—almost double his total from the Dead Ball Era—marking the official start of the Live Ball Era.

With the introduction of the live ball, Babe Ruth transitioned from an exceptional pitcher to the "Sultan of Swat," paving the way for the emergence of the Yankee Dynasty.

Ruth benefited from a new baseball produced in Australia, featuring higher-grade yarn made from wool or a wool blend. This tightly wrapped yarn surrounded a small cork core, resulting in a ball weighing between 5 and 5.25 ounces and measuring 9 to 9.5 inches in circumference.

Five years later, Milton Reach patented the "cushion cork center," which consisted of a core surrounded by black rubber and an additional layer of red rubber. This innovation provided Major League Baseball with a ball that allowed power hitters to send the ball soaring out of the park.

Further modifications continued to favor power hitters, including the outlawing of the spitball, the replacement of scuffed balls, the lowering of the pitcher's mound, improvements in field conditions, and the repositioning of outfield fences closer to the infield. Collectively, these changes marked the beginning of the Live Ball Era.

With this shift, the age of power hitters was born, a force that remains dominant in the game today. For many fans, nothing is more thrilling than witnessing a game-winning home run.

Meanwhile, pitchers lost many advantages they had during the Dead Ball Era. They could no longer rely on a rubber-core ball until it became dirty and hard to see, nor could they "doctor" the ball.

Nonetheless, pitchers retained the unique properties of the 108 raised stitches on the baseball. When gripped by a skilled pitcher, the ball can exhibit remarkable characteristics.

This grip creates low-resistance turbulent flow, enabling pitchers to execute extraordinary pitches. A pitcher's control over the stitches, combined with their arm and wrist movements, determines the ball's trajectory—whether it curves down, slides, rises, drops, or hops.

With the advantage of red stitches and the occasional use of a roughed-up or wet ball, pitchers maintain a significant edge over batters. On average, a major league hitter fails to achieve a hit about 73.5 percent of the time.

However, the dynamic changes dramatically with the home run. A single blast over the fence can dismantle a pitcher's carefully planned strategy, a phenomenon exemplified by Babe Ruth.

Ruth ruled the first 18 years of the Live Ball Era, but he would not have reached legendary status, nor would the Yankees have established their dynasty, without Jacob Ruppert. Ruppert was a successful businessman and politician who played a pivotal role in the team's history.

As a brewing company owner, Ruppert served in the United States Congress from 1899 to 1907 and attained the rank of Colonel in the New York Army National Guard.

In 1915, he purchased the New York Yankees, who were then playing at the Polo Grounds at Coogan's Hollow, in Upper Manhattan. Built in 1890, the Polo Grounds featured a distinctive bathtub-shaped field with short left and right fields and a deep center field. A promontory near the western shore of the Harlem River in Washington Heights overlooked the stadium.

At the time of Ruppert's acquisition, the Yankees were struggling and consistently overshadowed by the New York

Giants. Two years later, in 1917, he hired Hall of Fame manager Miller Huggins, who had previously managed the St. Louis Cardinals.

In 1919, Ruppert struck gold by acquiring Babe Ruth from the Boston Red Sox. He went on to construct Yankee Stadium, which opened in 1923, and signed Lou Gehrig in the same year. Together, Ruth, batting third, and Gehrig, hitting fourth, formed one of the most potent power-hitting duos in baseball history.

Gehrig boasted an impressive lifetime batting average of .340 and hit 493 home runs. He was a seven-time All-Star, a two-time American League Most Valuable Player, and a three-time American League home run leader. He played in six World Series, all won by the Yankees—four during Ruth's tenure and two after his departure in 1934. Gehrig was inducted into the Hall of Fame in 1939.

Ruth hit 714 home runs over his career and maintained a .342 lifetime batting average, alongside a pitching record of 94 wins and 46 losses. He was a 12-time American League home run leader and a five-time American League RBI leader.

Ruth won four World Series titles with the Yankees and three as a pitcher for the Boston Red Sox. He was among the first five players inducted into the Hall of Fame in 1936.

Though Ruth and Gehrig were both left-handed hitters, they had little else in common. Ruth grew up in an orphanage, while Gehrig attended Columbia University and played baseball for the school. Gehrig was soft-spoken, well-mannered, and non-controversial, whereas Ruth's life was more tumultuous, characterized by womanizing, heavy drinking, and a fiery temper. Ruth was a spectacle in his own right, constantly making headlines.

Standing 6'2" with broad shoulders and slender legs, Ruth swung at the ball with a powerful uppercut. In contrast,

Gehrig was stout and strong, renowned for hitting line drives. Babe Ruth has often been attributed with mystical powers. Legend has it that when he was sold to the Yankees in 1920, the Bambino placed a curse on the Boston Red Sox, as they didn't win another pennant for 86 years.

A legendary moment occurred on October 1, 1932, during a game against the Cubs at Wrigley Field. In the fifth inning, Babe Ruth famously pointed to center field and hit a home run, a moment that has since been immortalized as the "called shot."

Ruth transcended baseball, becoming America's most famous figure as radio and movies gained popularity, and symbolizing the nation's strength. Despite his character flaws, he earned titles like "The Sultan of Swat" and "The Bambino," solidifying his status as one of baseball's most iconic figures.

Although Ruth had a complicated relationship with teammate Lou Gehrig, he shared a strong friendship with Yankees owner Jacob Ruppert. Ruppert owned the team until his death in 1939, and Ruth was one of the last people to see him alive.

Ruppert had the foresight to capitalize on the talents of manager Miller Huggins, Ruth, Gehrig, and DiMaggio, investing significantly to build a strong team around them. He was the first owner to place numbers on the backs of uniforms and established a robust farm system. He also built Yankee Stadium, laying the foundation for a Yankee dynasty that would endure long after his passing. Ruppert was posthumously inducted into the Hall of Fame in 2013.

* * *

While at the Yankee camp I enjoyed the films and my conversation with Gus Gussack about Ruth. But I was particularly excited to meet former Yankees who played with Mickey Mantle. I was 10 years old in 1951 when Mantle began his Yankee career and I saw him play in San Antonio. I also watched him on television, read countless stories about him, and following the daily Yankee box scores. I still have a collector's copy of the July 1965 issue of *Life* magazine featuring him on the cover.

Mantle played for the Yankees from 1951 to 1968, hitting 536 home runs with a .298 batting average and 1,509 RBIs. He was a 20-time All-Star and won the American League Most Valuable Player award three times.

Mantle participated in 12 Yankee World Series and won seven championships. He holds multiple World Series records, including most home runs, RBIs, extra-base hits, walks, and total bases.

During the camp, I met Joe Pepitone, a three-time All-Star first baseman who hit 219 home runs over 11 seasons from 1962 to 1973. In the locker room, Pepitone hollered "Hey, if Mickey Mantle could see you guys wearing number seven on your shirts, he would turn over in his grave."

Later, I asked Pepitone, "What can you tell me about Mantle?"

He replied, "I played with some of the greatest ballplayers in the world, but Mantle was the best. We joked around together, hung out, and had fun. We were pals, and that helped ease the pressure. We want you guys to feel the same way."

Pepitone recounted numerous tales of wild nights, and the practical jokes Mantle played on his teammates—drenching players with ice water while they showered, leaving small snakes in their lockers, and engaging in endless teasing.

One evening, I had the opportunity to speak with Johnny Blanchard, a catcher and outfielder who played for the Yankees during Mantle's era and was part of two World Series championship teams.

I asked him, "Was Mantle a good leader?"

He replied, "Mantle was the chairman of the board, much like Frank Sinatra was with the Rat Pack. He would occasionally overrule manager Ralph Houk. Once he made a decision, that was final."

I inquired, "Were you close friends?"

He responded, "Absolutely. One day, I went 0 for 4. After the game, he tapped me on the shoulder and said, 'Let's go eat and have a few drinks at Denny's Hideaway tonight.' We enjoyed roast beef, had a few drinks, and then a few more. It really lifted my spirits. Later, I lived with Mickey on and off."

I asked, "Was he as good with kids as Babe Ruth?"

He answered, "I suggested he take a break during a game against Kansas City, since we had an important three-game series against Baltimore approaching. He said, 'Johnny, how would you feel if you were a father who brought his son to see Mickey Mantle play?' So, he played."

I commented, "I'm sure you miss him."

He replied, "After the lights went out on Broadway, Mickey became a lonely person. He insisted that for all his road show appearances, Moose Skowron, Hank Bauer, and I accompany him. I do miss him."

I asked, "Did Mantle ever forgive Jim Bouton?"

Blanchard responded, "I don't think Mantle ever forgave him. After Bouton's book *Ball Four* was published in 1970, Mantle refused to speak to him for years. They may have had a conversation just before Mantle passed away in 1995."

Jim Bouton pitched for four major league teams from 1962 to 1978, finishing with a record of 62 wins and 63 losses. During his tenure with the Yankees from 1962 to 1968, he won two World Series games in 1964.

Bouton wrote a book that revealed the behind-the-scenes lifestyle of Yankees players—excessive drinking, chasing women, sharing obscene jokes, and using drugs, including himself.

He highlighted Mantle's heavy drinking, which caused some players to never forgive Bouton. While the book gained popularity, it exposed many inside stories that embarrassed both management and teammates.

The book was well-written, sold millions of copies, and became a landmark in American sports literature. *Time* magazine recognized it as one of the 100 greatest books since the magazine's inception in 1923.

Every day at camp, we played baseball, divided into eight teams competing in seven games over four days. Each team was assigned two former Yankee players as coaches. Tommy John, with 288 victories, and Graig Nettles, who hit 390 career home runs, shared their knowledge, blending advice with humor.

During one game, John remarked, "Too bad the hitter swung and missed that pitch—it took a bad hop."

Nettles advised, "If the ball looks like an aspirin to you outfielders, get the hell out of the way."

Thanks to our coaches' baseball wisdom and humor, we won the tournament with a 6-1 record, allowing us to connect with the Yankee tradition in a fantastic way.

When I got home, I called Bouton to tell him I was writing a book about the Men's Senior League. I asked him why he started playing senior hardball.

He replied, "One day in 1985, I drove by a game and felt the urge to play again. Baseball has always been a constant in my life, and I missed it. I've played for fun my entire career; my highest major league salary was just $7,000.

"Pitching connects me to my childhood. I always looked

forward to playing each summer and preferred the younger leagues. I've never felt my age, and I measure life by the things I cannot do. So far, in my 60 years, there have been few things I haven't been able to do."

I asked, "Have Yankee fans and players forgiven you for writing *Ball Four*?"

He answered, "It took a long time to mend those relationships. I was at Yankee Stadium in 1998 for the old-timers' game. When I jogged out to the sidelines, the crowd erupted in applause. It felt like I was finally released from the principal's office for throwing spitballs.

"Thirty years after writing a book that I thought would only be mildly controversial is a long time to wait for redemption. It felt great to be back at Yankee Stadium and hear the crowd's applause. It was nice.

"Life is good. Say 'hi' to my man Gary Bell."

I replied, "I will."

Gary Bell is also my friend. He graduated from Luther Burbank High School, located on the south side where I grew up. I met him when he was selling sporting goods after his major league career ended in 1969.

During his 12 seasons as a major league player, he won 121 games, had an ERA of 3.86, and recorded 1,378 strikeouts. He was a four-time All-Star.

While having lunch with Bell, I mentioned, "I talked to Jim Bouton about his book. He asked how you were doing and told me to say hi to my man Gary Bell."

Bell responded, "Bouton and I were teammates on the Seattle Pilots in 1969. We became good friends and had a lot of fun together. Just don't tell him I've had two heart attacks, two angioplasties, and one heart bypass operation."

I asked, "I read *Ball Four*. What did you think of it?"

He replied, "Bouton was working on that book while we played together. We were all young guys in our 20s, just trying to have fun and relieve the tension of competing in the major leagues. It was controversial back then, but now the book is well-regarded. I'm okay with it."

* * *

After the Mickey Mantle era, the Yankees only won two World Series (1977 and 1978) until shortstop Derek Jeter joined the team in 1995, leading them to five championships. They secured their first title in 1996, followed by three consecutive wins in 1998, 1999, and 2000, with another championship in 2009.

I believe the Yankee dynasty ended following the Jeter era. One reason is that navigating the expansive playoff system, which now includes eight teams from each league, requires a degree of luck. The playoffs consist of a three-game series followed by a five-game series, culminating in a seven-game series, which allows any team to get hot and potentially make a deep run.

Despite not winning a World Series since 2009, the Yankees remain the most valuable team in MLB. In 2024, they appeared poised to win another championship, but they lost four games to one against the Los Angeles Dodgers.

We will always remember the Yankee dynasty during the eras of Babe Ruth, Lou Gehrig, Joe DiMaggio, Mickey Mantle, and Derek Jeter. They account for 24 of the 27 championships the Yankees have won. Those 27 championships are still a MLB record. While the Yankee dynasty has faded away, I do not believe another team will ever match the Yankee record of 27 World Series championship.

*At Yankee camp with pitcher Tommy John (left), who won 288 games,
Tony Ferrara and Graig Nettles, who hit 390 home runs.*

6. THE CATHEDRALS OF
THE MAJOR LEAGUES

ON MARCH 24, 2009, I joined Ken Burns and Dayton Duncan at their table during a luncheon in San Antonio. Burns is the author of *Baseball: An Illustrated History*, and together they produced the PBS series on the sport's history.

As we sat down, Duncan asked, "People say you still play ball."

I replied, "Yes. I play in the Men's Senior Hardball League, striving to preserve amateur baseball, much like it was intended to be when men played on the Elysian Fields in Hoboken."

Duncan responded, "I'm glad you are helping to uphold the tradition of amateur baseball. As a public official, you must have inspired other men to play."

I said, "I hope so," and then I turned to Burns, saying, "I appreciate that Major League Baseball is building new retro parks, but it's a shame they've demolished historic ones. There are only two left: Fenway and Wrigley. In the preface to your book, you discussed Ebbets Field."

He responded, "I was born in 1953 in Brooklyn, just three years before the Dodgers left for Los Angeles and the stadium was torn down. I heard so many stories about the Dodgers and Ebbets Field.

"The stadium was built in 1913 in the Flatbush neighborhood of Brooklyn. It was an impressive piece of architecture, highlighted by a stunning 80-foot circular rotunda made of Italian marble, with a ceiling that rose 27 feet high at the center. Inside, the floor was intricately tiled to resemble the 108 stitches of a baseball, and a chandelier hung from twelve baseball-bat arms, each holding a globe shaped like a baseball."

I said, "Even though the Dodgers left, Ebbets Field should have been preserved."

He responded, "Yes. We have lost a lot of memories of the Dodgers—who were first called the Trolly Dodgers because a streetcar once ran in front of the stadium—then became known as 'Dem Bums' because it took them 40 years to win their first World Series in 1955. But fans loved them like Hilda, who would ring a cowbell while lively music played, and spectators marched about in excitement."

I said, "I saw an exhibit in the Hall of Fame that included her."

He said, "Did you know that Jackie Robinson's grave is just a few miles from where the field once stood. He broke the racial barrier at Ebbets Field in 1947, the most important event in baseball."

For over 70 years, the New York Yankees faced the Brooklyn Dodgers 22 times each season, with their final game against the Yankees occurring on September 24, 1957.

Three years after the Dodgers left, a ceremony marked the end of an era at Ebbets Field. "Auld Lang Syne" was sung as the last remnants of the park were demolished, erasing 44 years of memories from existence.

Frank Sinatra paid tribute to Ebbets Field in his song "There Used to Be a Ballpark."

In closing, Burns added, "You should check out the Mets' new ballpark opening next month. The exterior resembles Ebbets Field, and inside, there's a large rotunda like the smaller 80-foot rotunda at Ebbets Field, named after Jackie Robinson. His quote on the upper rim reads, 'Life is not important except in the impact it has on other lives.'"

I replied, "It's great to hear that the owner respects baseball's history. I'm looking forward to visiting the park. But unfortunately, the owners of Yankee Stadium are tearing down 'The House That Ruth Built.' They should have improved it instead of building a new ballpark."

I enjoyed my time with Burns and Duncan, learning much more about the game. I even had them sign my first edition of *Baseball: An Illustrated History*, written by Ken Burns and Geoffrey Ward and published in 1994, the same year the PBS series was released.

* * *

Although we lost Ebbets Field and then Yankee stadium in 2009 we should be grateful that Fenway Park and Wrigley Field still stand. Of the two, Wrigley is my favorite. Located on the historic grounds of the Chicago Lutheran Theological Seminary, it exudes a powerful spiritual ambiance.

Wrigley Field broke ground on March 4, 1911, and held its first game on April 23, 1914. Originally built for the Chicago Whales of the Federal League, it is a true gem. After the Federal League folded two years later, the Chicago Cubs played their first game there in 1916.

For over a century, Wrigley Field has served as a sanctuary for countless fans, providing a welcome escape from urban life. Here, they engage in the rituals and traditions of baseball, enveloped by a mystique that transforms the experience into a supernatural haven amid nature.

During my many visits, my wife Tracy and I would disembark from the commuter rail and wander through the neighborhood, appreciating its absence of parking lots. As a collector of first editions, I made a point to explore the local used bookstores, including Roscoe Books, Book Runner, and Raven's Books.

As game time approached, I navigated the lively sidewalks, passing bars filled with Cubs fans. After finishing their last drinks, they gathered beneath the iconic red marquee sign from 1934 at the entrance.

Inside, the ivy-covered brick outfield wall merges effortlessly with the surrounding nature, creating a truly unique outfield fence unmatched in Major League Baseball. Fans on the private rooftops behind the outfield fence enjoy the game from their elevated vantage point.

Experiencing this historic setting is truly special as I sit among devoted fans who supported a team that last won the World Series in 1908. They finally celebrated another championship 108 years later, in 2016.

While I'm there, I am fully present, captivated by the moment. I don't want to leave, and I eagerly anticipate my next visit. In a shared experience, fans forge connections not just with the players but also with family and fellow fans and unite in cheers for their team. In those moments, the fans truly become "ONE," an essential part of the whole experience.

Upholding the tradition of day game for 72 years, Wrigley Field was the last major league park to host a night game, which occurred in 1988. But the field still features a handheld scoreboard. In 2020, it was designated a National Historic Landmark.

No religious cathedral can rival Wrigley Field—the Cathedral of Baseball.

I fondly recall listening to Harry Caray's broadcasts during Cubs games. For the last 16 years of his career, he served as their broadcaster, renowned for singing "Take Me Out to the Ballgame" during the seventh inning and his iconic catch-phrase, "Holy Cow!" whenever a home run was hit.

On June 20, 2002, Tracy and I dined at Harry Caray's Italian Steakhouse, where his widow, Dutchie, graciously signed my book, *I Remember Harry Caray.*

Ignoring the tradition of Fenway Park and Wrigley Field, in the 1960s, 70s, and 80s, MLB constructed cookie-cutter stadiums featuring artificial grass, neglecting the sport's rich history. Ten ballparks used artificial turf, destroyed the inspirational experience of being surrounded by a natural landscape. The magical connection to the lore and tradition of baseball and Elysian Fields was severed, leaving the MLB ballparks in a state of artificial surroundings.

Finally, in 1992, one MLB team truly understood how to create a ballpark that blended history, spirituality, and nature's vibrant greens. I attended a game at Camden Yards in Baltimore during its inaugural summer.

As I walked along Eutaw Street, nestled between the park and the surrounding warehouses, I was captivated by the lively atmosphere created by a variety of delicious food vendors. The arched windows and ornate brick walls, adorned with intricate cornice work, were truly a visual delight.

Inside, I was greeted by the sight of lush green grass bordered by an outfield wall that evoked the straight standards of the former Ebbets Field. I strolled past picnic areas behind the distinctive two-tiered bullpen and admired the bronze sculptures commemorating six legendary Orioles whose jersey numbers have been retired.

At the inaugural game on April 3, 1992, the Orioles' star shortstop Cal Ripken Jr. remarked, "This may be the first game, but it feels like baseball has been played here before."

Known as the "Iron Man," Ripken played for 22 seasons,

shattering Lou Gehrig's record with an astounding total of 2,632 consecutive games. He was inducted into the Hall of Fame in 2007.

In May 2019, I had the opportunity to meet Ripken when he visited a Boys and Girls Club on San Antonio's east side to dedicate a baseball field partially funded by his foundation, which received matching donations coordinated by club president Angie Mock.

After the ceremony, a small group of us spoke with him. I took a moment to express my gratitude for his foundation, which pays tribute to his father, a member of the Orioles Hall of Fame.

He responded, "Dad spent 36 years with the Orioles organization as a player, coach, and manager. Most importantly, he was a great dad who helped my brother Billy and me become major league players."

Later, I discovered that my friend David Lesch had faced Ripken in high school, with Ripken playing for Aberdeen and Lesch representing John Carroll.

Ripken's father advised Warren Lesch that his son David should sign with the Dodgers. Following this guidance, David signed a contract that included funding for his college education. He later earned both an MA and a PhD from Harvard—indeed, sound advice.

Camden Yards inspired the design of several modern ballparks, yet none have captured the spiritual essence of baseball's past quite like Camden Yards. These parks, however, are incredible venues that evoke the spirituality of great cathedrals. I have visited the Neo-Gothic St. Patrick's Cathedral with its elegant spires, Florence's Santa Maria del Fiore adorned with green, pink, and white marble, San Marco Basilica in Venice showcasing Italo-Byzantine style, St. Stephen's Cathedral in Vienna with its striking Romanesque and Gothic architecture, and Germany's Cologne Cathedral.

Since Camden Yards, several new parks have been built, including Coors Field in Denver, Jacobs Field (now Progressive Field) in Cleveland, Chase Field in Arizona, Miller Park in Milwaukee, the New York Mets' stadium, the Yankee's new park, and the Astros' ballpark in Houston.

My high school friend, Billy Burge, served as chair of the Houston Sports Authority, which was responsible for building the new Astro's ballpark. They refurbished the historic 1911 Romanesque Union Station to serve as the main entrance. To commemorate the station, a full-size vintage locomotive runs along 800 feet of track atop the left-field wall. The ballpark also features a retractable roof and real grass.

These major league parks have sparked civic revitalization and rekindled the spirit of baseball's rich history. I feel a thrill whenever I'm in these grand cathedrals of baseball. However, with approximately 50,000 fans attending games, the atmosphere can feel less intimate.

My granddaughters Nicole Prosper and Jordan Nash, who live in Houston, are big Astros fans. I enjoy going to games with them, standing around observing the crowd as fans stroll through the stadium's corridors. At Astros games, fans wear team caps, shirts, or both. Some sport red and orange overalls, complemented by large orange Styrofoam cowboy hats. Families often walk together in a chain formation to keep their kids from getting lost. You can hear hawkers calling out to sell programs and drinks, while in the Astros' stores, three lines of customers await service from one of the ten cashiers. It's a bustling and exciting scene.

While MLB has done a great job of building great baseball cathedrals, sadly it has also brought professional baseball to the brink of destruction. The warnings from the boys of Elysian Fields have come to pass as greed has eroded the integrity of the game.

Wrigley Field, home of the Chicago Cubs.

7. GREED CORRUPTS

On June 17, 2009, I had the privilege of spending a couple of hours with Jacques Barzun in his home in San Antonio, when he was 102 years old.

Barzun was a distinguished historian who authored and edited over 40 books, covering a diverse range of topics from mystery novels and classical music analysis to histories of ideas and cultural studies. More importantly to our story, he also wrote several essays on baseball.

In 1954, when I was 13, Barzun wrote that baseball reflects the spirit and tradition of America. He believed the game embodied the concept of the commons—open, democratic, and deeply social. He wrote baseball is both graphic and choreographic, mirroring not only the sport itself but also the religious rituals that signal the arrival of spring.

His most famous quote, now displayed on a plaque in the Baseball Hall of Fame, states:

> *Whoever wants to know the heart and mind of America had better learn baseball, the rules and reality of the game.*

However, by the 1990s, Barzun had dramatically changed his view. He expressed disgust for baseball, revealing that he no longer followed the sport and felt ashamed of what had become of this cherished pastime. He described the game as a disaster, attributing its decline to greed.

This shift in perspective began with a series of MLB strikes, lockouts, and the steroid scandal. The first strike occurred in 1972, followed by lockouts in 1973 and 1976, another strike in 1981, and another in 1985, culminating in a lockout in 1990. The 1994-95 strike proved to be the most severe, resulting in 938 canceled games, including all playoffs and the 1994 World Series.

Before I could ask him about baseball, he inquired, "What book are you reading now?"

I replied, "Michael Korda's book, *Ike: An American Hero.*"

He responded, "When I was provost of Columbia University in 1948, I hired General Eisenhower to be president of the university. He served until 1953."

"That's amazing," I said. "Living history right here."

I then asked, "In the 1990s, you changed your mind about the merits of baseball, stating that greed ruined the game. Do you still believe that?"

"Yes," he answered. "MLB is ruining baseball. After all the strikes and lockouts, the Players Union has blocked every attempt to require steroid testing, while the owners sit around the table counting their money."

I replied, "You're right about MLB, but the spirit and tradition of baseball are still alive in minor league baseball. Amateur baseball thrives too—through Little League, high school, college, men's senior leagues, and thousands of softball leagues."

"Yes," he conceded, "but MLB dominates the airwaves and is defining what baseball has become. MLB will never return to the glory days before strikes, lockouts, and steroids."

I brought with me Jacques Barzun's magnum opus, *From Dawn to Decadence*, a comprehensive history of 500 years of Western cultural life, penned when he was 93. He inscribed it with the words: "To Nelson Wolff with admiration and appreciation. Jacques Barzun." My visit with him was unforgettable, and it remains a cherished memory. Barzun passed away two years later at the age of 104.

After our meeting, I found myself reflecting on the sentiments of amateur players who once competed at the Elysian Fields of Hoboken. They believed that players should not be paid, seeing money as a corrupting influence in a game that ought to provide a noble example for youth and fans. They were right, greed contributed to the player strikes and lockouts and the steroid scandal that ultimately led Barzun to turn his back on baseball.

These strikes and lockouts began after Marvin Miller was hired in 1966 as the first executive director of the newly established Major League Baseball Players Association. This union welcomed all players, managers, coaches, and athletic trainers associated with a Major League club via a signed contract.

Growing up in Brooklyn as a Dodgers fan, Miller graduated from New York University with a degree in economics in 1933. He worked with various unions before joining the United Steelworkers, where he became their principal economic adviser and assistant to the president.

In the same year that Miller was hired by the Players Association, he negotiated the first collective bargaining agreement with team owners. This landmark agreement raised player salaries, increasing the minimum from $7,000 to $10,000.

In 1972, Miller led the first strike in MLB history. That year, he also advised St. Louis Cardinals outfielder Curt Flood, who challenged the reserve clause that severely restricted players' rights to their contracted teams.

Miller counseled Flood against filing a lawsuit, believing he would not prevail. Flood lost when the Supreme Court ruled against him in June 1972. However, in 1974, Miller successfully used arbitration to eliminate the reserve clause binding players to their signed teams, resulting in a significant increase in player salaries.

Miller served as executive director until 1982, a tenure marked by numerous strikes and lockouts. Under his leadership, the average player salary surged from $19,000 in 1966 to $326,000 in 1982.

Miller was a transformative figure who wrested power from the owners, liberating players from their constraints and providing them with unprecedented wealth. Consequently, the Players Association has become one of the most powerful unions in the country.

Miller passed away on November 17, 2012, and was inducted into the Hall of Fame in 2020.

Miller laid the groundwork for his successor, Donald Fehr, who led the players' union during its most challenging strike. Fehr oversaw a 232-day strike from 1994 to 1995, resulting in the cancellation of 938 games, including all playoffs and the 1994 World Series. As a direct consequence of this strike, average player salaries skyrocketed from $400,000 to $3 million. Fehr served as executive director for 24 years.

At the same time that the strikes began, changes in baseball would lead to more home runs. In 1975, the ball's cover was switched from horsehide to cowhide. The new cowhide cover encases a cork nucleus wrapped in rubber, along with 121 yards of blue-gray wool yarn, 45 yards of white wool yarn, and 150 yards of fine Australian cotton yarn.

In Costa Rica, over 1 million baseballs are produced for Major League Baseball (MLB) each year. Artisans carefully hand-stitch the two-piece cowhide covers with exactly 216 double-raised red cotton stitches.

Studies show that MLB uses a livelier ball compared to the minor leagues, which employ balls made in China containing a cork-and-rubber composite. Tests conducted at the University of Massachusetts revealed that the major league ball can travel eight to nine feet farther than its minor league counterpart.

A test in 2000 indicated that major league balls have tighter yarn windings, which add an additional five feet to their travel distance.

While the lively ball benefited power hitters, MLB also began preparing 72 balls for each game, replacing them every sixth pitch. This policy resulted in cleaner balls, which could travel farther.

Throughout a season, approximately 227,000 balls are used, costing the league around $2 million.

In response to the increasing use of live balls, pitchers resorted to tactics reminiscent of the Dead Ball Era. Some skilled pitchers found ways to manipulate the ball, even though such practices were illegal.

Detroit Tigers pitcher Brian Moehler was caught with sandpaper in his glove and received a 10-day suspension. Joe Niekro was discovered with sandpaper in his back pocket, while Rick Honeycutt faced suspension for scuffing the ball with a thumbtack.

Infielders and catchers have occasionally scuffed balls on behalf of their pitchers. A pitcher might also inadvertently apply saliva or another wet substance to the smooth part of the ball, creating a downward spin upon release.

The increasingly lively ball and the use of 72 balls per game led to more home runs. Power hitters needed to be stronger to achieve high home run totals. Similarly, pitchers were required to be bigger and stronger to throw with extraordinary speed. Successful players stood to earn substantial financial rewards. The pursuit of glory and financial gain drove players to seek advantages, ultimately leading to one of the greatest scandals in sports history.

With the union's power equal to that of the team owners, baseball now had two organizations dominated by greed. The union coupled with the owners' complicity, led to a scandal that destroyed the credibility of MLB.

Since the early 1990s, many observers suspected that players were using steroids, pointing to noticeable increases in players' head and foot sizes, as well as their more muscular physiques.

MLB recognized that something was amiss but chose not to address the issue, as fans flocked to witness these oversized athletes hitting home runs. Both the owners and the enhanced players were reaping substantial profits.

*　*　*

On February 27, 2016, I joined former MLB player José Canseco at the Colt 45 Baseball Field on Applewhite Road in south San Antonio for a charity game benefiting veterans, with Canseco as the main attraction.

Canseco played in MLB for eight different teams, was named American League Rookie of the Year in 1986, and won the Most Valuable Player award in 1988. A six-time All-Star, he hit a total of 462 home runs before retiring in 2001.

In 2005, four years after his retirement, Canseco published a book titled *Juiced*, claiming that 85% of major leaguers used steroids and naming several players.

In the book, he admitted to using performance-enhancing drugs, saying these substances made him stronger and a better player. While he acknowledged the serious risks of steroid use, he argued that it was acceptable with proper medical guidance.

How misguided he was. Prolonged steroid use can lead to severe health issues, including cataracts, glaucoma, immunosuppression, muscle wasting, and bone changes. It can also cause fluid retention, exacerbate diabetes, and lead to Cushing's syndrome—a condition characterized by a round face and a hump between the shoulders.

The Colt 45 league had invited me to throw out the first pitch at the charity game. Upon my arrival, I was struck by Canseco's impressive physique, from his large head to his muscular build. While surprised, I understood why. He greeted me warmly with a big smile as I shook his massive hand.

While warming up with Canseco in the outfield, I asked him, "Why did you write *Juiced*?"

He replied, "Instead of covering up steroid use, I wanted to tell the truth. Why hide it when using them is fine if you have medical advice?"

I continued, "Do you regret writing the book?"

His response was, "No. I expressed the truth as I saw it."

During the game, Canseco hit a towering home run that thrilled the small crowd of about 100 fans. I kept a signed ticket from the game and placed it in my signed first edition of *Juiced*. As I left the ballpark, I reflected once again on Barzun's disillusionment with baseball. What drives players like Canseco to use steroids? They could have been exceptional athletes without resorting to such measures. The answer is simple: the relentless pursuit of greater glory and money has forever tarnished a significant era in baseball.

Canseco's retirement has been anything but smooth. Steroid use can cause personality changes, including sudden mood swings, which contributed to his two arrests for domestic violence, assaults on tourists in Florida, and citations for reckless driving while armed with a loaded semi-automatic weapon.

As Canseco has aged, his excessive steroid use has impaired his body's ability to produce testosterone naturally. By 2023, he appears much older and weaker than his actual age, struggling to maintain a livelihood through celebrity boxing, semi-professional leagues, and martial arts.

The first public indication of steroid use emerged in late 1998 when reporter Steve Wilstein discovered an open container of androstenedione in the locker of St. Louis slugger Mark McGwire. That same year, McGwire hit 70 home runs, breaking Roger Maris's record of 61.

Barry Bonds seemed unable to tolerate the attention McGwire was receiving. For Bonds, being great was not enough; with his enlarged head, feet, and muscular physique, he hit 73 home runs in 2001, driven by a desire for fame and fortune.

The following year, in 2002 the BALCO scandal erupted as a federal investigation began into the company. This investigation revealed that the San Francisco Bay Area lab supplied anabolic steroids to various athletes, including Barry Bonds. In 2003, American League MVP Jason Giambi admitted before a grand jury to using steroids obtained from BALCO.

In response to these revelations, Congress passed the Anabolic Steroid Control Act in 2004, classifying anabolic steroids and prohormones as controlled substances, making possession a federal crime. That same year, the United States Food and Drug Administration prohibited the sale of androstenedione.

In 2005, coinciding with the publication of *Juiced*, a congressional hearing on performance-enhancing drugs was held. Senator John McCain stated that baseball could not be trusted and emphasized the need for federal legislation to clean up the game.

In 2006, former Senator George Mitchell launched a 20-month investigation into the use of anabolic steroids and human growth hormone among major league players. The resulting 409-page report, released in 2007, detailed the history of illegal performance-enhancing substances and named several players, including one of baseball's greatest pitchers, Roger Clemens, who won 354 games, received seven Cy Young Awards, and was an eleven-time All-Star.

In contrast, a pitcher as remarkable as Roger Clemens—or perhaps even greater—did not use steroids. Throughout his 27-year career, Nolan Ryan achieved 5,714 strikeouts, setting a Major League Baseball (MLB) record. He is the all-time leader with seven no-hitters and is tied for the most one-hitters. Ryan won 324 games, earned eight All-Star selections, clinched a World Series championship, and is one of only 31 players to have competed in four different decades. He was inducted into the Hall of Fame in 1999.

A congressional report on steroid use highlighted the players' union's refusal to cooperate, which hindered efforts to combat steroid use and stalled the implementation of an effective random testing program.

The financial interests of baseball players and owners further contributed to the issue of steroid use. Today's minimum salary is $740,000, and the average MLB player earns nearly $4.88 million—a figure skewed by the exorbitant salaries of superstar players.

On January 10, 2013, more than 15 years after Mark McGwire was caught using androstenedione, MLB and the players' union finally reached an agreement on a comprehensive random testing program that included stringent penalties for noncompliance, such as suspensions from baseball.

Unlike Major League Baseball, the National Football League (NFL) began testing for steroids in 1987, issuing suspensions the following year. The National Basketball Association (NBA) initiated its steroid testing in 1983 and strengthened its program during the 1990s.

Many prominent players implicated in steroid use, including Barry Bonds, who hit 762 home runs during his career, Mark McGwire, who hit 593 home runs, and Roger Clemens, who won 354 games, have not been elected to the Hall of Fame. When Hank Aaron graciously congratulated Bonds, I find myself wishing he hadn't. Aaron is the true home run champion. He concluded his 24-year career (1954-1976) with 755 home runs. He boasted a lifetime batting average of .305, accumulating 3,771 hits and 2,297 runs batted in. Aaron also enjoyed an illustrious career as a 25-time All-Star and was named National League MVP in 1957.

Aaron was the last former Negro League player on a major league roster and was inducted into the Hall of Fame in 1982. He passed away in 2021.

Baseball prides itself on meticulous record-keeping dating back to the first published box scores in 1859. The game is rooted in statistics—balls, strikes, putouts, errors, stolen bases, singles, doubles, triples, home runs, batting averages, earned run averages, and many other metrics are closely monitored.

For over 150 years, these statistics have allowed us to compare players across different eras. However, the steroid era has severely distorted our historical understanding of baseball.

Since Major League Baseball and the Players Union took action against steroid use, no player has come close to matching the impressive home run totals achieved by Mark McGwire and Barry Bonds.

* * *

While MLB was addressing the steroid scandal, another controversy arose in 2017. During that year's seven-game American League Championship Series against the New York Yankees, the Houston Astros won four games at home but lost three on the road. In the World Series, the Astros split the first four games at Dodger Stadium before winning two out of three games at home.

In November 2019, reporters Ken Rosenthal and Evan Drellich revealed the Astros' sign-stealing scheme. Mike Fiers, a pitcher for the Astros in 2017, confirmed that cameras played a significant role in this operation.

Before the Astros' sophisticated tactics, the most famous alleged sign-stealing incident, though legal at the time, was documented in the book *The Home Run Heard 'Round the World*.

In 1951, the New York Giants and the Brooklyn Dodgers entered the final game of the season tied. The Dodgers led 4-1 going into the ninth inning. With one out and two runners on base, Giants player Bobby Thompson hit a walk-off home run off Dodger pitcher Ralph Branca.

It was alleged that the Giants employed someone in their clubhouse, located in center field, who used a telescope to steal signals. At that time, sign stealing was not prohibited by MLB, and it wasn't until 1961 that the league banned the use of optical or mechanical devices for this purpose.

On a related note, I own a first edition of *The Home Run Heard 'Round the World,* written by Ray Robinson, which is signed by Bobby Thompson, Ralph Branca, and Monte Irvin.

As technology advanced in the early 2000s, more sophisticated and foolproof methods for stealing signals emerged. During the 2017 and 2018 seasons, the Astros utilized cutting-edge technology for this purpose.

They installed a video camera in their field house, located in center field, which could zoom in and clearly capture the opposing catcher's signals to the pitcher. The video feed was transmitted to a monitor in the locker room, where staff members watched live and conveyed signals to the players by banging on a trash can to indicate the upcoming pitch.

A silence indicated a fastball, while one or two bangs signaled a curveball. It's fascinating how technology combined with the simple act of banging a trash can proved to be an effective method.

How did baseball reach a point where nearly everyone in the Astros organization, including many players, was aware of their unprecedented cheating in a clear violation of the 1961 prohibition?

I believe this culture of cheating stemmed from the Astros' drive to win at any cost, which began with Jeff Luhnow's hiring as general manager in 2011. An engineer, management consultant, and technology entrepreneur, Luhnow leveraged his business acumen and technological insights to foster this new culture within the Astros.

He reduced the staff by half and recruited a new team of software engineers, statisticians, and Wall Street analysts. Within just three years, he turned a struggling organization into world champions.

He took the principles of *Moneyball* to new heights. *Moneyball* refers to the book by Michael Lewis, which chronicles how Oakland Athletics General Manager Billy Beane began using sabermetrics to evaluate player performance starting in 1997.

Luhnow had an advantage over Beane in measuring player performance due to modern technology like Trackman. This system offers comprehensive in-stadium coverage, enabling complete tracking of a ball's flight and measuring critical metrics such as exit velocity, spin rate, and launch angle. This wealth of information is invaluable for assessing potential players.

Luhnow excelled at restructuring the Astros' staff and evaluating player performance which was a tremendous achievement. But he also introduced an incentive program that motivated staff members to prioritize winning above all else. For example, the head of technology, who reportedly had an annual salary of $40,000, received $450,000 in bonuses after the Astros won the World Series.

However, the relentless pursuit of victory ultimately led to cheating. I believe the Astros had a strong enough team to succeed without resorting to dishonest tactics.

When the scandal emerged in 2019, MLB Commissioner Bob Manfred initiated an investigation. The resulting report revealed that the Astros had used a video camera to steal signals.

As a consequence, the Astros were fined $5 million and stripped of their first and second-round draft picks for 2020 and 2021. Additionally, Manfred suspended Astros General Manager Jeff Luhnow and Field Manager A.J. Hinch for the 2020 season. Shortly after the report's release, Astros owner Jim Crane dismissed both men.

Despite their involvement in the scandal, no players faced fines or suspensions, a decision that former Commissioner Fay Vincent criticized. Manfred later acknowledged that this was not his best decision.

While advancements in technology facilitated the elaborate signal-stealing scheme, subsequent innovations are trying to ensure that such cheating will not happen again.

Catchers can now use transmitters resembling wristbands, equipped with nine buttons corresponding to different pitch signals. By pressing a button, the catcher's signal is transmitted verbally to the pitcher, who hears it through a 6-inch rubber receiver embedded in his cap. MLB approved the use of these devices in 2023.

* * *

In 2024, I published a book titled 95 *Power Principles*, drawing from my experiences as a State Representative, State Senator, San Antonio City Councilman, and Mayor, as well as my 22 years as Bexar County Judge. One of the principles, "Refuse to dance with sports hustlers, the handmaidens of Beelzebub (the devil)," was inspired by the underhanded tactics of the Miami Marlins.

In November 2005, I received a call from John McHale Jr., the vice president of Major League Baseball. He informed me that Marlins President David Samson was interested in visiting San Antonio.

McHale expressed that the Marlins might relocate to another city due to their last-place attendance, and he was unable to secure assistance from Miami for building a new stadium.

At that time, as Bexar County Judge, I had overseen the construction of the county arena, which opened in 2003 and serves as the home of the San Antonio Spurs basketball team. So, I was excited about overseeing the building a new major league stadium.

In December, Samson and two of his staff members visited San Antonio. I presented a plan to secure up to $200 million for a new stadium, and they seemed impressed.

In mid-February, Samson contacted me to indicate their intention to relocate. He said, "We're assessing your market and would like to meet with you sooner rather than later."

As news of a potential relocation to San Antonio spread,

Nolan Ryan reached out and met with me in my office to offer his support. Afterward, I networked with other investors and secured commitments from several companies for advertising and ticket sales.

On March 2, the Miami Herald reported that Major League Baseball President Bob DuPuy indicated San Antonio had become the focal point in discussions about the Marlins' potential relocation.

Samson visited San Antonio to evaluate the proposed stadium site along IH-35 on the city's north side. We set a deadline to finalize the deal by May 15.

Later, Samson called to explain, "It's going to take us two weeks or longer to assess the stadium proposal, prepare a media package for broadcasting games, and gather economic data on San Antonio. We need Major League Baseball to concur with our assessment. If that report is favorable, I want to come to San Antonio and not leave until we have a deal."

This raised a red flag for me; the delay and conditions felt suspicious. I expressed my disappointment about the postponement and made it clear that I would not keep the offer open past the agreed deadline of May 15. I followed up with a letter stressing that the Marlins needed to make their decision by that date.

On April 3, Mayor Hardberger and I accepted an invitation from Samson and his stepfather, Jeffrey Loria, the owner of the Marlins, to attend the team's opening game against the Astros in Houston.

While returning home, I received a call from DuPuy. He said, "I understand you're under time constraints. We'll focus on San Antonio and strive to complete our work by May 15."

A few days before the deadline, Samson requested an extension, but I refused. After investing over four months into this effort, I discovered that the Marlins had no intention of leaving Miami. Years later, they built a new stadium in the city, yet their attendance remains among the lowest in the league.

This situation exemplifies greed—manipulating one city against another in a dishonest manner. I can partially blame myself for being deceived; my passion for baseball blinded me to their falsehoods.

It is disheartening to see what MLB and the Players Union have done to the game of baseball with strikes, lock outs, steroids, cheating, and lying. Millions of fans have turned away from MLB, and the game is no longer the nation's pastime.

The World Series, once the greatest American sporting event ever, has seen its viewership plummet from 44 million per game during the 1978 showdown between the Yankees and Dodgers to approximately 15 million today.

MLB had high hopes that the 2024 World Series, featuring the Dodgers and Yankees again would reignite interest among a dwindling television audience. These two storied franchises boasted a combined annual player payroll of around $650 million, partly due to the absence of a salary cap in baseball compared to other major sports.

The payrolls of both teams included five MVP award winners: Dodgers Shohei Ohtani, Freddie Freeman, and Mookie Betts, along with Yankees Aaron Judge and Giancarlo Stanton. Additionally, Juan Soto, a runner-up for the MVP, further enriched this star-studded lineup.

Adding to the anticipation was Aaron Judge's incredible performance during the 2024 regular season, where he led the major leagues in home runs, RBIs, on-base percentage, and boasted an impressive .332 batting average.

However, the series did not meet expectations for those hoping it would rekindle fan interest like the 1978 World Series.

Despite featuring two of baseball's wealthiest teams with marquee players, the games only drew an average of 15.8 million viewers on Fox—roughly one-third of the 44 million who tuned in for the 1978 series.

In comparing the MLB World Series to the NFL Super Bowl, the disparity is stark. The February 2025 Super Bowl between the Philadelphia Eagles and Kansas City Chiefs attracted 126 million viewers. The Fox broadcast network averaged 111.5 million viewers, while its streaming service added another 13.6 million. An additional 800,000 watched on NFL digital services. If the number of baseball fans who tuned in for each World Series game were the same fans, the Super Bowl would have had about nine times more viewers.

According to published reports, ESPN officials informed MLB officials that their baseball television rights were declining in value. ESPN had been paying $550 million a year, an amount that had already been reduced substantially in the past.

ESPN opted out of the last three years of the contract, saying the rights were only worth $200 million a year. MLB Commissioner Manfred declined the offer, ending a 35-year partnership

Because of no salary cap and the right for teams to create local media rights has led to the dominance of major market teams like the Los Angeles Dodgers and New York Yankees, creating a huge disparity among teams.

MLB continues to be its own worst enemy, leading to a continuing media fan base.

To reestablish baseball as America's pastime, MLB should take inspiration from Japan, where the sport thrives as the national passion. American expatriates introduced baseball to Japan in 1859, following the country's opening of ports to trade. By 1872, it began being played in high schools.

Professional baseball emerged in Japan during the

1920s, gaining significant traction in 1934 when Babe Ruth led an all-star team on a tour of the country.

The Nippon Professional Baseball League, established in 1936, is divided into the Pacific and Central Leagues and serves as Japan's equivalent to Major League Baseball (MLB). Over the years, 64 Japanese players have made the transition to the majors in the United States.

Throughout my political career, I participated in several trade missions to Japan. In 2003, I successfully led an initiative to establish a Toyota manufacturing plant in San Antonio, which now provides employment for over 8,000 workers, including their supplier companies.

During my time in Japan, I attended a game at Meiji Jingu Stadium in Shinjuku, Tokyo, the home of the Tokyo Yakult Swallows. This iconic stadium, which opened in 1926, hosted a historic game in 1934 when an American team featuring legends like Babe Ruth, Lou Gehrig, and Jimmy Fox faced off against Japanese teams.

Baseball holds a significant place in Japanese culture, embodying values such as hard work, group identity, and corporate spirit. Fans show their unwavering dedication by chanting and dancing to team songs, creating an electrifying atmosphere in stadiums filled with passionate supporters.

In contrast to the United States, where greed and corruption have tarnished the sport, Japanese baseball remains largely unscathed by issues like gambling, cheating, and performance-enhancing drugs. The professional league has experienced only one strike in its history, lasting just two days.

The 2023 World Baseball Classic highlighted this devotion, with the matchup between Japan and Korea attracting an impressive 65 million viewers, making it the most-watched baseball event in history.

In the final against the United States, Japan was leading 3-2 with two outs in the ninth inning when pitcher Shohei Ohtani faced his Los Angeles Angels teammate, Mike Trout. Both players are considered generational talents. With a full count, Trout swung and missed at a slider thrown low and away, securing Japan's victory and their title as World Champions. Over 55 million viewers watched this thrilling game.

Major League Baseball (MLB) has been unable to dispel the belief held by its founders that money could corrupt the pure amateur spirit of the game, once played in the Elysian Fields of Hoboken. It is hoped that MLB and its players have learned from past mistakes and will move forward without allowing greed to tarnish the sport anymore.

Professional baseball played in the minor leagues does not have the rich trappings of Major League Baseball. As a result, Minor Leagues has not been tarnished by major scandals and exemplifies the best of professional baseball.

Regardless of MLB's trajectory, baseball will endure as a beautiful game, played in various venues—from Little League and high school to college and semi-professional leagues, to sandlot games and senior leagues, encompassing both fast-pitch and recreational softball. Baseball will continue, timeless and unyielding.

Photograph: San Antonio Express-News

Jacques Barzun

8. THE CHAPELS OF
THE MINOR LEAGUES

IN 1964, THE MISSIONS won both the regular season and playoff titles in the Texas League, achieving the league's first double championship in eight years. However, what should have been a joyous celebration turned into a challenging time for professional baseball in San Antonio.

At that time, the San Antonio franchise and Mission Stadium were owned by the Houston Colts, who sold the team to a business group from Amarillo, Texas. While they kept ownership of Mission Stadium, they prohibited any professional teams from using it, aiming to avoid competition with their Houston team.

Two years later, in 1966, I graduated from St. Mary's University School of Law with a business degree and a Doctor of Jurisprudence.

The following year, I received a call from Elmer Kosub, the coach of the St. Mary's baseball team, which has a rich history dating back to 1902. Notably, in 1910, the team won all its games except for an exhibition match against the Detroit Tigers, led by Ty Cobb.

Today, St. Mary's competes in NCAA Division II as a member of the Lone Star Conference, boasting 24 conference titles and four appearances in the Division II NAIA College World Series.

Kosub had been coaching the St. Mary's team since 1957, leading them to 15 conference championships and an appearance in the Division II NAIA World Series in 1976.

He said to me, "I have some good news. The university will provide land on our campus for a new ballpark for the St. Mary's baseball team and a proposed minor league franchise."

In response, I said, "That sounds exciting. Hopefully, we can secure a new franchise."

He continued, "I want you to become a founding member of a nonprofit organization, the San Antonio Sports Association. If we build a new stadium and are willing to manage the franchise, we will secure a Double-A franchise."

"I would love to be involved," I replied.

We formed a 19-member Board of Directors that included notable figures such as Tom Murrah, President of Jefferson State Bank; former major league player Arthur Veltman; St. Mary's Coach Elmer Kosub; City Manager Gerald Henckel; Manuel Calderon; and Henry Christopher.

We secured a new Double-A franchise with the Chicago Cubs, contingent upon the construction of the stadium, and signed a lease agreement for the land with St. Mary's.

We built the stadium on a spacious green field behind the academic buildings, facing 36th Street and surrounded by towering trees, creating a picturesque setting. Our family business, Alamo Enterprises, provided the building materials and used our trucks to transport salvaged lights collected by Kosub from an abandoned stadium in Dallas.

The Houston Colts permitted us to remove bleachers, seats, and turnstiles from the now-defunct Mission Stadium. The stadium was a mere shadow of its former self and was ultimately dismantled, with the land sold off.

After completing the new stadium, we fulfilled the

Chicago Cubs' requirements for establishing a Double-A franchise in San Antonio, and our volunteer group took over its management. We served as ushers, ticket takers, and concession stand helpers.

The stadium's inaugural game, an exhibition match between the Cubs and the White Sox, took place on March 31, 1968, attracting a crowd of 4,500 fans.

It was thrilling to watch Ernie Banks, the Cubs shortstop and a 14-time All-Star, 2-time MVP, 2-time National League home run leader, and Hall-of-Famer who was also named to the Baseball All-Century Team. He passed away in 2015 at the age of 83.

An interesting footnote is that my friend Steve Schramka's father, Paul, had a brief stint with the Cubs in 1953. He was the last player to wear number 14 before Banks took it, a number that has since been retired in Banks' honor.

On April 16, the Missions hosted their inaugural game before a crowd of 3,000 fans, averaging about 1,000 attendees per game throughout the season.

After our sports association managed the franchise for three years, we transitioned it to private ownership in 1971. Given the minimal profits in minor league baseball, ownership was primarily driven by a passion for the game.

Attendance received a significant boost in 1980 when pitcher Fernando Valenzuela was promoted to our Double-A team. He was one of twelve children from Etchohuaquila, Mexico, and had been pitching for the Leones de Yucatán when a Dodgers scout discovered him and signed him for $120,000.

My friend David Lesch met Fernando during Spring Training at Dodger Town in Vero Beach earlier that year, before Fernando arrived in San Antonio. Both signed contracts with the Dodgers, with Lesch being the number one draft pick at just

19 years old.

Dodger Town was unique as a training ground for both major and minor league players, allowing them to live and work together on the same grounds.

Lesch recalled, "Fernando couldn't speak much English, but I was reasonably good at Spanish, so we managed to communicate. He was a nice, humble guy whom I initially underestimated because he wasn't tall and lanky like most pitchers. Boy, was I wrong."

Lesch could have pitched for the Missions in 1982 if he hadn't torn his rotator cuff that year. He is now a Distinguished Professor of Middle Eastern history at Trinity University and has published 18 books.

I witnessed Fernando pitch his famous screwball, a delivery that left hitters stumbling in their attempts to make contact. He dominated the Texas League by securing 13 victories with a 3.10 ERA and leading the league with 162 strikeouts.

Fernando's outstanding performance earned him a promotion by the Dodgers at the end of the season in San Antonio. In 1981, he became a larger-than-life figure, winning both the NL Rookie of the Year and the NL Cy Young Award, igniting the fan phenomenon known as "Fernandomania."

Throughout his 17-year MLB career, he recorded 173 wins with a 3.53 ERA, was selected as an All-Star six times, pitched a no-hitter on June 19, 1990, and received the Silver Slugger award twice, often stepping up as a pinch hitter.

It's unfortunate that he has not yet been inducted into the Hall of Fame, as he was the first great Mexican American player.

The year after Valenzuela's standout season, Orel Hershiser was promoted to Double-A ball to join the Missions team. He spent two seasons in San Antonio but garnered little attention, primarily working as a reliever.

Hershiser went on to enjoy a successful 17-year career in the major leagues, earning 204 wins with a 3.48 ERA. He won the NL Cy Young Award in 1988 and was named an All-Star three times.

Nineteen years after the inaugural Missions baseball game at St. Mary's Field, I was elected to the San Antonio City Council in 1987. That same year, Burl Yarbrough was hired as the General Manager of the Missions and later became president in 2000.

Yarbrough grew up in Fort Worth, Texas, and graduated from the University of Texas at Arlington, located just a few miles away, with both a BBA and a master's degree.

He began his career in minor league management, arriving in San Antonio from the Myrtle Beach Blue Jays. Over the next 38 years, during which he managed the franchise, Burl and I became good friends.

Burl inherited the franchise during a challenging period for minor league baseball. The 1980s were particularly tough, with nationwide attendance plummeting from over 42 million in 1949 to less than 10 million.

Part of the reason was a lack of fan-friendly ball parks. Burl and I recognized our existing facility was in poor condition.

In 1987, the same year I was elected to the city council, *Bull Durham* was released. I recognized the profound impact that films can have—they inspire dreams, ignite imagination, and evoke deep emotions. Engaging with these stories activates multiple regions of the brain, especially during emotional moments, shaping our attitudes and behaviors.

Many of us have been captivated by films that transport us to fictional worlds, inspiring us to turn our dreams into reality. I hoped that *Bull Durham* would rekindle interest in minor league baseball and motivate our community to create a new ballpark.

In the opening scene, Annie Savoy, played by Susan Sarandon, stands before her baseball shrine, reciting a poem about the church of baseball that resonated deeply with me.

She recites:

I believe in the church of baseball,
I have tried all the major religions
And most of the minor ones.
I have worshiped Buddha,
Allah, Brahma, Vishnu,
Siva, trees, mushrooms.
I know things.
For instance, there are 108 beads
In a Catholic rosary,
And there are 108 stitches in a baseball.
The Lord laid too much guilt on me.
I prefer metaphysics to theology.
You see, there's no guilt in baseball,
And it is never boring.

Annie's vision of the church of baseball as a space free from guilt and full of vibrant experiences profoundly impacted me. It inspired the sanctuary I envisioned creating—a spiritual haven for both fans and players.

In the film, Annie shows her devotion to the Durham players by granting special favors to those who achieve a batting average of over .250.

She also psychoanalyzes the struggling rookie pitcher, Ebby Calvin "Nuke" LaLoosh, played by Tim Robbins. By boosting his confidence, she reassures him that his lack of self-awareness will help him become a great pitcher.

Annie encourages "Crash" Davis, the seasoned minor

league catcher portrayed by Kevin Costner, to advise LaLoosh that overthinking could hinder both his performance and the team's success.

We cheered when LaLoosh was called up to the majors and celebrated as Davis broke the minor league home run record. We delighted in the antics of Max Patkin, the Clown Prince of Baseball, who entertained fans at the charming and historic Durham Bulls ballpark until his passing in 1999.

After watching the movie, I reached out to Miles Wolff (no relation), the owner of the Durham Bulls Baseball franchise, to learn more about the film's origins and its effect on his team.

He shared, "I received a call from a friend who asked if Kevin Costner could use the ballpark for a film. I agreed. When Costner arrived, I met him at the field and promised to do everything I could to help make his movie a success. We provided crowds for the shoot, ballplayers as extras, and all the necessary equipment."

"As filming progressed," Wolff recalled, "I thought Costner was making a terrible movie. The crew changed their opinions daily—first wanting a crowd for a daytime game, then switching to a nighttime game. As a minor-league owner, I was appalled by the waste of money and time. By the end of the three-week shoot, I thought it would be a miracle if the film ever made it to the screen."

After the film's release, I quickly recognized that something special had unfolded in Durham. "After the release, we sold a huge amount of Durham Bulls merchandise," Wolff noted.

He added, "Other minor-league clubs also saw increased sales. Each city aimed to establish its own identity, distinct from its major-league affiliate. As a result, more people across the nation began attending minor-league games, thanks to the movie."

Bull Durham captured the imagination of baseball fans, encouraging them to rediscover the joy of family outings to smaller minor-league ballparks and igniting renewed interest in these venues. The film inspired cities and counties to build new, fan-friendly parks.

Many baseball enthusiasts plan vacations around visits to minor-league parks, seeking a spiritual experience. My late friend Jim Dublin visited 37 minor-league parks during his travels.

He would say, "I take along my Baseball America schedule, which lists the schedules for both minor and major league teams. Upon arrival, I check into the motel where the visiting team stays."

"I prefer to arrive at the ballpark an hour before the game, allowing me to be the first to buy a beer and explore the park. I savor the unique essence of each park—their sights, sounds, and smells. Each one is an architectural gem." As Jim observed, "They all have their own unique identity. They are homey, friendly places without pretensions."

Once the fans arrive, the park springs to life with people who love baseball. They seem to know one another, like friends gathering for a celebration. They even applaud the opposing team and don't leave in anger if their team loses.

The fans in Medicine Hat, Alberta, Canada, were particularly entertaining. I attended a noon businessman's special, where the franchise owners provided fans with fake noses and glasses as disguises so their bosses wouldn't discover they were at the game, creating a lively atmosphere.

After hearing Dublin's stories and watching *Bull Durham*, I felt inspired to seek council support for creating a small, intimate chapel-like ballpark. I envisioned a park that would evoke an uplifting spiritual feeling similar to what parishioners experience in the thousands of small chapels across the country.

San Antonio is home to the oldest cathedral in the United States, San Fernando Cathedral, whose cornerstone was laid in 1734. This Gothic-style structure features intricately carved stone Stations of the Cross, stunning stained-glass windows, and two prominent spires. It serves as the mother church of the Archdiocese of San Antonio and the seat of its archbishop.

In 1831, James Bowie married Ursula de Veramendi in this church, which also holds the ashes of the Alamo heroes who died during the 1836 battle.

Located in the heart of San Antonio, San Fernando Cathedral overlooks Plaza de las Islas, a historic site where early settlers established their homes. Today, adjacent to the cathedral, stands the City Council chambers, a building constructed during my tenure as mayor, facing the plaza. Directly across from the cathedral is the Bexar Courthouse, where I served as County Judge for nearly 22 years, from 2001 to 2022.

The Archdiocese of San Antonio also oversees chapels in each of the four historic missions: San José, San Juan, Concepción, and Espada. These four historic chapels, located on the grounds of the Missions, each have vibrant congregations. I believed that the spirituality of these chapels could be replicated in a chapel like a minor league ballpark.

Many individuals feel empowered to define God according to their personal beliefs, seeking spirituality outside of traditional organized religion. They crave meaningful connections with nature and friendships that allow them to share meals and experiences.

Being part of a community positively impacts both health and well-being. For example, a study at the University of Kansas found that sports fans experience lower levels of depression, and a stronger sense of belonging compared to non-fans.

I recognized the importance of emotionally connecting with our community. Our emotional intelligence drives our actions, helping us achieve our goals; it enhances our understanding of our own feelings and those of others, reinforcing positive memories and stimulating beneficial brain responses. My goal was to rekindle a love for baseball and the serene atmosphere it represents.

A baseball chapel surrounded by lush green fields would foster a unique spirituality. The ballplayers are up close to the fans much like a preacher is to his parishioners. In such a small baseball chapel all the fans can support one another, cultivating deep friendships as they watch and cheer for their team.

Inspired by the film *Bull Durham*, I continued to advocate for a new ballpark. I brought it up so often that the *San Antonio Express-News* featured a cartoon of a farmhouse under a puzzled moon.

Inside, a voice mused, "We could plow down the cornfield and build a ballpark with VIA funds from the Alamodome, and then we...."

At that moment, Tracy interjected, "Nelson, go to sleep."

Despite my efforts as a councilman, I struggled to gain support, which led me to run for mayor in 1990, making the ballpark a central issue in my campaign.

After my election as mayor in June 1991, I intensified pressure on my fellow council members to endorse the new park. Using baseball metaphors to evoke emotions, I would say things like, "You hit a home run," "You're the cleanup hitter," "You're on deck," "You need to swing for the fences," and "You're a major leaguer."

I played catch with them on the front lawn of City Hall and invited them to participate in the charitable fundraising games I organized. Additionally, Tracy and I took city council members to Mission games to showcase the park's poor condition.

In 1992, Kevin Costner starred in the baseball film *For Love of the Game*, which follows an aging Detroit Tigers pitcher as he faces the intense pressure of pitching in Yankee Stadium.

To calm himself, he reflects on his long-term relationship with his girlfriend, Jane Aubrey. In the final inning of what could be a perfect game, he signs a baseball for Wheeler and says, "Tell them I am through. For the love of the game."

He ultimately pitches a perfect game, but that night, alone in his room, he weeps for the loss of baseball and for Jane, the other love of his life. The film concludes on a poignant note, capturing the bittersweet reality that every baseball player confronts when their final game ends.

The same year the film was released, I discovered a stunning 40-acre tract of land featuring trees and expansive green spaces reminiscent of the Elysian Fields in Hoboken. This land was located just southwest of downtown and across Highway 90 from Camargo Park.

I reached an agreement with the Levi Strauss family to sell the land to the city for 40 cents per square foot, totaling $17,460 per acre—a true bargain.

After acquiring the land, I persuaded the City Council to allocate $10 million for a new ballpark, joining over 50 other cities that constructed minor league parks during the late 1980s and 1990s.

Before breaking ground on our ballpark, Tracy and I aimed to experience spring training in Florida, where major leaguers play in minor league stadiums, hoping to draw inspiration for our own park.

The modern era of spring training began in 1948 when

the Dodgers established Dodger Town in Vero Beach. While Florida remains home to many training camps, ten teams now conduct their spring training in Arizona. Spring training symbolizes hope and renewal for players striving to improve their performance or secure a roster spot.

Fans from across the nation flock to Florida and Arizona to support their favorite teams. Attending these games evokes the spirit of minor league matchups, where the outcome is secondary, and the focus rests on preparing players for the regular season.

We chose to watch the Houston Astros play a spring training game at Osceola County Stadium in Kissimmee, Florida. Next to us sat the wife of Astros outfielder Daryle Ward, who had just been called up from Triple-A. She expressed her anxiety about his performance, but he ultimately secured a spot on the Astros' roster.

During the game, we spoke with their owners, Drayton McLane and his son-in-law, Bob McClaren, about the possibility of the Astros holding a preseason game in San Antonio. McClaren was enthusiastic about the idea.

After the game, I shared with Tracy how much I enjoyed being close to the field, where I could witness the players' remarkable skills.

She replied, "Skills are great, but I appreciate their great-looking buns."

It's clear that everyone has their own reasons for wanting to watch a game up close.

Later, we attended a Tampa Bay Devil Rays game at Florida Power Park, which overlooks the bay in St. Petersburg.

Back home, we boarded a private plane with our architects and visited four minor league parks in one day, taking notes at each location. While each park had its unique merits,

I emphasized to the architects my desire to create a distinctive space that combined a religious atmosphere with a fan-friendly environment.

Later the architects presented a design featuring two neo-mission-era revival towers at the entrance of the park, which I imagined as a small baseball chapel.

With a seating capacity of 6,500—compared to the 50,000 seats found in a major league stadium—the park offered an intimate atmosphere that brought fans closer to the action. We made sure to incorporate picnic tables along the outfield sidelines, allowing children plenty of room to run and play catch. A large grassy berm behind left field provided a perfect spot for fans to spread out blankets and relax. We also landscaped the surrounding area with grass, shrubs, and trees.

Yarbrough ensured that the playing fields remained in excellent condition for the players. Between the white foul lines, the players enjoyed a green oasis.

The ballfield faced southeast, allowing the summer's prevailing winds to cool the spectators. Additionally, the setting sun would be behind the stadium, keeping it out of the fans' eyes and enhancing the park's appeal as a pitcher's haven—a feature I had always valued.

Construction was completed on time and under budget. On April 18, 1994, we celebrated the grand opening. That night, 9,336 fans attended the game between San Antonio and El Paso, marking the largest attendance in Texas League history.

Inside the park, I included church-like sculptures, relics, alcoves, shrines, and sanctuaries. One alcove showcased a sanctuary honoring the saints of Mission baseball's past, featuring sculptured metal portraits of Hall of Fame third baseman Brooks Robinson, second baseman Joe Morgan, and All-Star pitchers Orel Hershiser and Fernando Valenzuela, all with roots in San Antonio.

As a nod to religious relics, we also sold artifacts, such as photographs, uniforms, and baseballs.

During the seventh inning, we stood together and sang:

Take me out to the ball game.
Take me out with the crowd.
Buy me some peanuts and Cracker Jack.
I don't care if I never get back.

The lyrics, penned by Jack Norworth in 1908, serve as baseball's beloved anthem, celebrating the sport's rich traditions.

Our cozy minor league ballpark, equipped with fan-friendly amenities, is a haven for families and friends to enjoy the relaxed pace of the game and connect with one another. Regular attendees form friendships with ushers, attendants, and vendors.

Fans appreciate their time together as much as they do watching the games. While indulging in hot dogs and cold beers, they engage in lively conversation and laughter. Some lounge under umbrellas on the grassy berm behind left field, enjoying family picnics.

The Missions' mascot, "Henry the Puffy Taco," entertains children by racing around the bases between innings, and after the game, kids get the chance to run the bases themselves. The players stay post-game to sign autographs, fostering a warm family atmosphere.

In their inaugural season, 411,959 fans attended the games, setting a Texas League attendance record. These fans came to watch young athletes play for modest salaries, regardless of the Missions' wins or losses, all while dreaming of making it to the Big Show.

Our park provides a spiritual experience where families and friends feel safe, happy, and secure as they soak in the atmosphere. It offers a refuge from life's chaos. Watching the players perform an unscripted ballet on a natural stage, we find ourselves enveloped in an idyllic setting, much like parishioners in a welcoming space.

Throughout the years, I have attended numerous games, but one memorable day stands out. In late April 1999, I attended a daytime doubleheader at Wolff Stadium, where the Missions faced the El Paso Diablos. We sat in field-level seats, positioned close to the action.

Frost Bank Vice President Pat Frost and his friends played "mound ball," with each contributing a dollar to a pot. They took turns holding the money at the end of each half-inning, and if the ball landed on the mound, the holder won the pot.

Fans wore T-shirts, shorts, or blue jeans, with many sporting baseball caps or straw hats. Kids filled the area, playing catch on the sidelines and running on the grassy berms while their parents relaxed with hot dogs and cold sodas or beers.

I can't attend a game without enjoying a hot dog, the quintessential staple of American baseball. This tradition began when German immigrants introduced frankfurters to the U.S. in the 1800s. I'm not alone in this preference—19.1 million hot dogs were sold at MLB games in 2022.

During a lull between games, the sound system played "Rock and Roll, Part Two" by Gary Glitter. The music created a mellow ambiance as I watched the ground crew cut, drag, and water the infield grass, restripe the baselines, and rework the pitcher's mound and batting box.

Two girls wearing fish fins on their feet raced while dribbling beach balls. Some players signed autographs, while others ran wind sprints or stretched nearby. A pickup truck drove along the warning track, advertising its price and display-ing brightly colored ads for local businesses.

The Missions won the first game but lost the second; however, for most fans, the outcome didn't matter. After the game, all the kids eagerly ran the bases.

It was a simple, homey, and unpretentious setting where everyone felt at ease. Conversations flowed as we watched young men play this highly skilled game of baseball, and we left feeling spiritually enriched after a heartfelt three-hour experience.

Yarbrough has hosted numerous special events over the years, including fireworks at every Saturday night game and a car giveaway on used car night. He has also organized baseball bat and cap giveaway nights, among many other activities.

After I left the office, the Mission ballpark was named in my honor. Nelson Wolff Municipal Stadium was recognized by *baseballparks.com* as one of the best minor league parks in the nation. Over time, sportswriters began to refer to it as "The Wolf." Some hitters even dubbed it "The Big Bad Wolf" due to the challenging prevailing winds. Nevertheless, the wind keeps fans cool, and pitchers appreciate it.

By 1998, we ranked 29th in attendance among 174 minor league teams across the United States and Canada, a notable achievement given that many communities were building new minor league stadiums.

That same year, an impressive 35,427,012 people attend-ed minor league games, a significant increase from a low of 10 million in the late 1980s. This rise occurred with only 174 teams, in stark contrast to the 464 minor league clubs in 1949.

On April 3, 1999, fulfilling a promise from Astros owner Drayton McLane, the Houston Astros visited Wolff Ballpark to face the Detroit Tigers. They invited me to play in the outfield during batting practice before the game.

Astros star Jeff Bagwell hit a towering home run and afterward expressed newfound respect for the dedicated fans who passionately supported the Astros. The players embraced the minor league experience, with one even tackling Puffy Taco at the end of an inning. Approximately 9,000 fans attended the game.

In 2004, ten years after we opened Wolff Stadium, a miracle happened. Michael Miller and his wife Yvette were advised that their expected child would have Down syndrome and that Yvette should consider terminating the pregnancy. They chose to have their child, who turned out to be perfectly healthy. Sydney Faith is now a junior at TCU with a 3.9 GPA.

When I recently spoke with Michael, he shared, "God blessed us with a healthy daughter, and I wanted to do something to help people with special needs. I decided to create a baseball league where children with special needs in the Bexar County area could play on a field designed for them. I played baseball in high school in Eagle Pass and made the all-district team. Hitting, running, and playing catch bring everyone together like no other sport."

I reached out to my friend Jesse James Leija, who helped me raise several million dollars for our non-profit, "The Miracle League of San Antonio." We successfully built a ballpark next to Wolff Stadium, where hundreds of individuals with special needs—ranging from young children to older adults—have enjoyed playing.

Michael Miller's efforts to bring baseball to those who might not otherwise have the opportunity are truly inspiring. Today, there are over 400 Miracle League fields across the nation. The spirit of baseball and nature impacts our lives; we just need to reach out, as Michael did.

Meanwhile, fan attendance at minor league parks has continued to rise. By 2019, minor league teams attracted

41,504,776 fans, nearing the record high of 42 million set in 1949 and a significant increase from the 10 million low observed during the 1980s.

New parks across the nation have played a crucial role in revitalizing fan attendance. Communities have returned to modern facilities in their hometowns, rediscovering a connection to simpler times filled with strong values. Families can enjoy a wholesome environment for an affordable, pleasant evening of baseball, indulging in nostalgic favorites like Cracker Jack, soda pop, cold beer, and hot dogs.

You may have wondered what happened to the ballpark at St. Mary's University, where the Missions played from 1968 to 1994. For several years, the stadium we built continued as the home of the St. Mary's baseball team.

In 2008, as County Judge, I included $4 million in a bond package and later added another $2 million for the University to build a new stadium for baseball and a new stadium for girls' fast-pitch softball. Additional funds were raised, and both stadiums were constructed.

In the next chapter let's turn to the Negro Leagues, which had a significant presence in my hometown. The leagues struggled due to a lack of financing. MLB's white oligarchs not only prevented black players from joining MLB but also failed to invest in the Negro Leagues. African Americans were left to navigate a racist society on their own.

Board members of The San Antonio Sports Association.

At our ballfield with Gary Bell (39) standing behnd me.

Pitching – as Mayor – on the lawn outside City Hall, trying to build support for a new ball park, 1993 (note improvised pitching mound!).

Wolff Stadium, home of the San Antonio Missions.

9. THE NEGRO LEAGUES

DID YOU KNOW THAT Moses Fleetwood Walker was the first black man to play in the major leagues? Surprisingly, he played for the Toledo Blue Stockings in the American Association in 1884, a league recognized by MLB as a major league. This was Walker's only season in the majors, and he remained the last black player in Major League Baseball for 63 years until Jackie Robinson broke the racial barrier in 1947.

While black players could not participate in the majors, a few competed in the minor leagues between 1883 and 1898. It is estimated that around 55 black players played in the minor leagues during this time.

The International Minor League provided the most opportunities for black players. Some participated on white teams, while others were part of black teams competing within the minor leagues.

As a result, nearly all professional black players participated in various Negro leagues. The National Colored Baseball League was founded in 1877 but quickly failed.

For several decades, different Negro leagues came and went. One independent league operated in San Antonio, featuring several black teams, including the San Antonio Broncos, Black Aces, Black Indians, and Porters. They played many games at Electric Park when the Texas League team was out of town.

During my campaign for Texas State Representative

in 1970, I spoke with Valmo Bellinger, the publisher of the San Antonio Register, the most successful African American newspaper in the Southwest. His father, Charles, managed the San Antonio Black Bronchos.

In 1905, Charles signed Joseph Williams, who was born in Seguin, Texas, approximately 30 miles from San Antonio. Over the next five years, Williams achieved impressive pitching records for the Black Broncos: 28-4, 15-9, 20-8, 20-2, and 32-8.

In 1908, with Williams on the mound, the Black Broncos won the state championship. He earned the nickname Smokey Joe Williams thanks to his remarkable skill against batters.

When I asked Valmo about Smokey Joe, he reminisced, "I was 11 years old when he pitched his last season for my dad. He was tall and lanky, standing at 6'4" with long arms. His fastball was unlike any other. My dad would use two catchers during games because Smokey's pitches would cause the first catcher's hand to swell from the impact. He was the best pitcher ever, whether in Negro ball or Major League Baseball."

I inquired, "Did you follow his career after he left San Antonio?"

Valmo replied, "Yes. In 1910, he was picked up by the Chicago Giants, one of the top teams in Negro Baseball. Barred from playing in the major leagues because of his color, he continued to excel, playing 22 seasons in the Negro leagues before ending his career with the Detroit Wolves."

Our shared passion for baseball created a strong connection, and Valmo supported my campaign for State Representative, which I won.

In 1952, 31 baseball experts came together to select the greatest black players from 1910 to 1952. Smokey was voted the top Negro pitcher, receiving more votes than anyone else, including Satchel Paige. Hall-of-Famer Ty Cobb remarked that

Smokey would have undoubtedly won 30 games in Major League Baseball.

During postseason barnstorming exhibitions, Smokey posted a 20-7 record against major league teams, defeating Hall of Fame pitchers Grover Cleveland Alexander, Walter Johnson, and Rube Marquard. Notably, he threw a no-hitter against the New York Giants in 1917—the same year the Giants secured the National League pennant.

Despite his remarkable achievements, Smokey never had the chance to play in Major League Baseball. Throughout his career, he earned very little money and struggled to find restaurants and motels that would serve him. Nevertheless, he loved the game and remained a hero to African Americans.

Smokey Joe's legacy has lingered like a phantom in baseball history. During his lifetime, he did not receive the recognition he deserved, unlike contemporaries such as Rube Walker, Josh Gibson, Cool Papa Bell, and Buck Leonard. In San Antonio, few knew of him, despite his induction into the San Antonio Sports Hall of Fame. As a point of interest, I was also inducted into that Hall of Fame.

Finally, 48 years after his passing, Smokey was recognized by Major League Baseball and inducted into the National Baseball Hall of Fame. Many other black players from the Negro Leagues would eventually receive acknowledgment from MLB as well.

My friend John "Mule" Miles, born in San Antonio in 1922, played for the Chicago American Giants in the Negro big leagues. His playing days came after Smokey Joe's career. After returning to San Antonio in the 1960s, he played for the Black Sox in the Negro bush league.

He earned the nickname "Mule" from his manager because he hit the ball with remarkable force, as if it had been kicked by a mule. In 1948, he hit 27 home runs for the Chicago Giants.

One day, I asked him about facing Satchel Paige.

"Did you hit against Paige?" I inquired.

"Yes," he replied. "He was hard to hit because his ball had incredible movement—a slow curve, changeup, and a fastball that would move to the outside of the plate. He had many ways of releasing the ball, including his famous hesitation pitch."

Miles played alongside many legendary players in the Negro Leagues, such as Jackie Robinson, Josh Gibson, and Hank Aaron. He was inducted into both the Texas Black Sports Hall of Fame and the San Antonio Sports Hall of Fame.

I had the opportunity to meet with Deborah Omowale, CEO of the San Antonio African American Community Archive and Museum. Joining our conversation were members of her team. During my term as County Judge, we provide $5 million in funding for the museum.

We talked about the South Texas League, a semi-professional league, that was founded in 1945. The league played games at Black Sox Stadium, Pittman-Sullivan Park, and at Mission Stadium from 1945-1979.

Former Negro League players including John "Mule" Miles, Roy White, Bernard Willis, and Cleveland Grant, played in the league. In the 1960s and 70s, major league players included Cliff Johnson (New York Yankees), Odie Davis, (Texas Rangers), and Cito Gaston (San Diego Padres and World Series Manager of the Toronto Blue Jays).

In 1999, the San Antonio Missions hosted a special night at Wolff Stadium to honor players from the Negro Leagues. Among those in attendance were Carl Long (Birmingham Black Barons), Jimmy Dean (Philadelphia Stars, New York Black Yankees, and New York Cubans), Ira McKnight (Kansas City Monarchs), and my friend John "Mule" Miles (Chicago American Giants).

I spoke with Ira McKnight, a five-time Negro League All-Star, who reflected, "I loved playing baseball in the Negro League. It formed a brotherhood that has lasted my entire life. I believe I would have played in the major leagues if I'd been given the chance, but I also don't think I could have been any happier."

I asked, "I hear you caught Satchel Paige."

He replied, "I caught Paige when he was 47 years old. I aimed for a target low enough for the batter not to see it. I didn't give him any signals; I just positioned my glove where I wanted him to throw, and he hit it. He still had great control."

Paige began his career with the Birmingham Black Barons in 1927 and gained national prominence in 1946 when Hall -of-Famer Bob Feller organized a barnstorming tour, fielding a major league all-star team and inviting Paige to lead a team of Negro League players.

Paige's team held its own against Feller's, even defeating them several times. In postseason games against major league players, Negro leaguers achieved an impressive record of 309 wins out of 438 games.

By the time the Cleveland Indians signed Paige to a major league contract in 1948, he was already a national figure. At 42 years old, he made history as the oldest rookie to debut in the majors. That season, he recorded a 6-1 win-loss record, including two shutouts and a low 2.48 ERA. He also participated in the 1948 World Series, successfully pitching two-thirds of an inning in the series that the Cleveland Indians won.

After his release from Cleveland, Paige played for the Philadelphia Stars in 1950. This independent Negro team existed from 1933 to 1952. He also played in both the Negro National and American Leagues.

In 1965, at age 59, Paige returned to the mound, pitching one game for the Kansas City Athletics. He was relieved in the fourth inning and received a standing ovation.

In 1971, Paige was inducted into the Hall of Fame, becoming the first Negro Major League player to receive this honor. He passed away at age 75 in 1982 in Kansas City.

One of the best teams in the Negro Leagues was the Cuban Giants, who played from 1885 to 1915. Despite their name, there were no Cubans on the team; it was comprised of light-skinned Black players. By calling themselves "Cuban," they became more acceptable to the public.

Some independent Negro professional teams also competed against college and minor league teams, while others played in the short-lived Middle States and Connecticut leagues. These teams were among the first fully salaried Negro teams.

The first successful Negro League was founded by Rube Walker, who established the Negro National League in 1920. Frequently referred to as the father of Black Baseball, Walker was not only the manager of the New York Black Giants but also one of the top pitchers of the early 1900s.

* * *

In September 2017, I met with Pacific Coast League President Branch Barret Rickey III at Wolff Stadium. Barret is the grandson of Branch Rickey, the man credited with breaking the MLB color barrier by signing Jackie Robinson.

Our meeting was prompted by a press conference announcing that our Double-A Mission team would transition to Triple-A baseball starting in the 2019 season. While I was excited about this change, I was even more eager to discuss his grandfather's legacy.

I turned to Barret and said, "I have a great admiration for your grandfather. Why did he take the controversial step of breaking the color barrier?"

He replied, "Because he had a strong moral foundation. He graduated from Ohio Wesleyan University, which was based on the principle of 'The Liberality of local people.' The university opposed slavery in the early 1850s, advocating for equal rights for all, regardless of skin color."

"After college he served in the army during World War I, leading a chemical training unit that included Ty Cobb and Christy Mathewson."

"How did he begin his baseball career?" I asked.

"After the war, he managed the Cardinals for six years. He was later hired as president and general manager of the Brooklyn Dodgers. By 1943, he owned 25% of the Dodgers, giving him the authority to break the color barrier."

"He began searching for the 'right man'—a player who could endure racist remarks from fans and opponents while positively representing his race. He ultimately found this right man, Jackie Robinson who was playing for the Kansas City Monarchs."

The Kansas City Monarchs are widely regarded as the greatest team in the Negro National League. As the longest-running franchise in the league, they secured ten league championships and won the inaugural World Series in 1924. From 1920 to 1962, they produced more Major League players than any other Negro franchise.

Barret continued, "Before playing baseball for the Monarchs, Robinson was a standout football player at UCLA. He was drafted into the military during World War II. He was court-martialed for refusing to move to the back of the bus but was eventually honorably discharged. My granddad liked that he stood up for what was right.

"When Robinson joined the Dodgers, he made it clear he wanted fair treatment. My grandfather assured him that the team would support him, but he emphasized that Robinson would need to be strong enough to ignore the racist slurs from fans and opposing players."

I commented, "Your grandfather had an exceptional ability to judge character. Robinson was an important figure for both America and baseball. Did you spend a lot of time with your grandfather?"

He replied, "Our family lived nearby, so I often visited him. I learned a great deal from him about both baseball and life. We were very close."

I added, "I understand your dad was also a baseball executive. Did he work with your grandfather?"

He responded, "Yes. My dad was the farm system director for the Brooklyn Dodgers while working alongside my grandfather. They were two of my best friends.

"I unfortunately lost my dad when I was 15, and then, four years later, my grandfather passed away. I still miss them both very much."

I expressed my condolences and remarked, "It's remarkable that three generations—your grandfather, your dad, and you—have built successful careers in baseball, spanning from 1935 to today. That's over 82 years, and you're still going strong."

He replied, "You might be surprised to learn that many people don't even remember my grandfather, let alone what my dad and I have achieved."

I said, "It's hard to believe that anyone connected to baseball wouldn't know about your grandfather. I saw the film '42' about Jackie Robinson. Did you have any involvement in it?"

He answered, "No, I declined. I did so out of respect for

Rachel Robinson, Jackie's widow. I didn't want to overshadow Jackie with a story focused on my grandfather. I attended the premiere and thought the movie was excellent. Harrison Ford did a great job portraying my grandfather."

Branch Rickey was inducted into the Hall of Fame in 1967, two years after his death. I felt fortunate to have such a meaningful conversation with his grandson.

Robinson played first base for the Dodgers in his debut game on April 15, 1947. He had a stellar career with the team, earning the National League Rookie of the Year award in 1947 and the National League batting title in 1949. He was a six-time All-Star with a lifetime batting average of .313 and 141 home runs.

Inducted into the Hall of Fame in 1962, he is buried in Cypress Cemetery, near the former site of Ebbets Field.

Despite Robinson breaking the racial barrier in baseball, discrimination remained widespread across the country.

I take pride that in my hometown of San Antonio when seven lunch and cafeterias peacefully integrated in on March 16, 1960. This peaceful integration was in contrast to protest and violence across the south.

Afterwards Jackie Robinson was quoted in several national newspapers saying: "San Antonians are setting examples for our whole nation." He later came to San Antonio and spoke at two churches.

Although we are a mid-sized city, our annual Martin Luther King march attracts more participants than any other city in the United States.

Finally, in 1964, when I was 23 years old, President Lyndon Baines Johnson led the effort to honor President Kennedy's legacy by passing historic civil rights legislation. He succeeded in signing it into law on July 2, 1964, just over seven months after Kennedy's assassination.

This landmark civil rights law outlawed discrimination based on race, color, religion, sex, and national origin. It prohibited racial segregation in schools, employment, and public accommodations. The law honored our fallen president and marked a new chapter in the lives of minorities.

In 1971, as a freshman member of the Texas House, I cast my vote for the Equal Rights Amendment to the United States Constitution, with Texas being among the first states to ratify it. I also had the opportunity to meet President Johnson, who expressed his pride in our state's ratification of the amendment. It has taken a long time for our country to recognize that the color of one's skin does not define who we are. Even after the passage of civil rights legislation, discrimination continued to persist in the southern states.

While Jackie Robinson broke the color barrier in baseball, it was Willie Mays who captured the hearts of all Americans. Mays was the greatest player to emerge from the Negro League, ultimately becoming one of the best major league players in history.

One day, I spoke with Skip Bradley, the president of the Senior League team I played for, and I asked if he had ever seen Willie Mays play baseball in Birmingham, Alabama, where he had grown up.

"Yes," he replied. "My father took me to a game in 1948. That year, Willie Mays began his professional career at 17 with the Birmingham Black Barons. They played at Rickwood Field, the oldest professional baseball park, built in 1910."

I inquired, "How did he perform?"

"He was exceptional right from the start. He helped his team reach the Negro League World Series against the Homestead Grays, although they lost the series 4-1."

I asked, "How long did he play there?"

"I believe it was just one year. The Black Barons played at the park from their first game in 1924 until 1960. Many years later, when I participated in a senior league tournament at the field, I used Willie Mays's old locker. In 2024, MLB held a game there to honor its historic significance."

As a cheerful team leader, Mays chose to lead by example rather than speak out against discrimination, earning him admiration from all. He became a unifying figure. Mays began his career with the New York Giants in 1951, just four years after Robinson broke the color barrier.

One of his most famous moments came in 1951 when Mays caught a line drive hit by Pirate Rocky Nelson at his knees with his bare hand in deep center field at Forbes Field. Then, in the first game of the 1954 World Series, he made a phenomenal catch over his shoulder while sprinting to the Polo Grounds center-field warning track off a hit by Cleveland slugger Vic Wertz.

Mays was a 23-time All-Star with a lifetime batting average of .301, amassing 3,293 hits and 669 home runs. He was a five-tool player, renowned for his strong arm, exceptional fielding, speed on the bases, and ability to hit for both power and average.

In 1999, *Sporting News* ranked the 100 greatest players of all time, placing Mays second to Babe Ruth, although many believe he should have claimed the top spot.

In 1969, MLB recognized players from seven Negro leagues as equivalent to major league players. In 2020, they added six more leagues to this recognition, which led to the acknowledgment of statistics for approximately 3,400 players who competed between 1920 and 1948—the year after Jackie Robinson broke the color barrier.

As of 2022, 37 black players, managers, and executives have been inducted into the Hall of Fame, largely due to their contributions to the Negro Leagues.

In 2024, Major League Baseball (MLB) began officially recognizing the statistics of Negro League players from 1920 to 1948 alongside those of MLB players. Notably, Josh Gibson's lifetime batting average has now surpassed that of Ty Cobb, earning him the distinction of having the highest average.

While we have made significant strides in racial relations, baseball deserves acknowledgment for its role in this progress, even if it came late in the game.

Let's now turn to women playing ball. They had to struggle to gain the right to play organized ball, facing discrimination in a different way than African Americans.

All images via Wikimedia Commons

Above: Smokey Joe Williams

Above right: Jackie Robinson

Right: Willie Mays

10. WOMEN PLAYING BALL

WHEN I SERVED AS MAYOR, Pepper Paire Davis, an all-star catcher who played in the All-American Girls Professional League, visited me on July 1, 1992. During the league's existence from 1944 to 1954, over 600 women participated across 10 teams, drawing more than 900,000 fans to their games.

I welcomed a petite 68-year-old woman who beamed with a smile, still retaining the same spark she had when she began her baseball career at the age of 20.

I said, "Congratulations on your remarkable career. Most catchers struggle as hitters, but you drove in 400 runs over your career, tying for fourth place."

She replied, "I always performed better under pressure, especially when a teammate was on base. I focused on hitting line drives to bring in runs."

I then asked, "I know you played semi-pro softball before joining the baseball league. How did you transition from softball to hardball?"

She responded, "I grew up with baseball. My older brother taught me the game, so I had experience with hardball before I played softball."

I continued, "Did you enjoy the movie *A League of Their Own*, starring Tom Hanks as the manager of one team? It has just premiered."

She said, "Yes, I love it. I served as a technical advisor to director Penny Marshall. The movie features the official song of our league, which I co-authored. Our victory song goes like this: 'We come from cities near and far. We're all for one, we're one for all.'"

I really enjoyed our visit. She signed a photo of herself in her catcher's gear, writing, "To Nelson, as mayor, you're in a league of your own."

Later, in 2009, she published a book titled *Dirt in the Skirt,* which included a foreword by Tom Hanks. She is also honored in the "Women in Baseball" exhibit at the Baseball Hall of Fame. She passed away in 2013 at the age of 88.

Pepper Paire Davis and the women who played in the All-American Girls Professional League owe a debt of gratitude to Annie Gibbons, who entered Vassar College as an orphan in 1865. Fortunately, she inherited wealth from her father allowing her to go to Vassar, one of only seven Ivy League institutions for women at that time.

During her second year at Vassar, Gibbons helped establish the Laurel and Abernakis Baseball Club, which consisted of two teams of nine women each.

She thoroughly enjoyed playing baseball and once wrote to her brother John, "We think after we practice a little, we will let the Atlantic Club (men) play a match with us."

The women players had to provide their own uniforms and played on a rough field hidden from the rest of the school, as society disapproved of women participating in baseball. Numerous newspaper articles claimed that playing baseball undermined feminine sensibilities and posed health risks.

Due to societal pressure, the school was urged to disband the women's baseball club, resulting in the dissolution of both teams the following year.

Annie later became the valedictorian and president of

her graduating class before earning her medical degree from a school in Ann Arbor, Michigan.

Thanks to a research team from Vassar, we have a rich collection of Annie's writings, including numerous letters and notes detailing her experiences.

In July 1874, she married lawyer Frank Houts, who later turned to ranching and moved Annie and their three daughters to Decatur, Texas. In 1882, she and her children joined Frank on a cattle drive along the Chisholm Trail, where she kept a journal documenting encounters with Indians flooded river crossings, and storms that struck their tents.

Annie's remarkable life took a tragic turn in 1888 when she hanged herself from a rafter in a closet upstairs while her children played on the first floor.

With colleges closing their doors to women playing baseball, women began forming their own teams. Notable among them were the Springfield teams, the Blondes and the Brunettes. Black women also established their own teams, and over the next three years, more than 20 organized women's teams were founded across the nation.

* * *

Two years after my visit with Davis, in June 1994, I received a call from Mission President Burl Yarbrough.

He asked, "Mayor, how would you like to play a game against the Colorado Silver Bullets?"

I replied, "That's an easy yes. I hear they just started playing."

Burl explained, "Yes, they will tour the country, playing against men's teams comprised mostly of former major and minor league players. Notably, former major league players Bob Bruce and Cliff Johnson have agreed to join our team."

I asked, "When is the game scheduled?"

He replied, "July 30 at 7:00 p.m."

I was thrilled about the chance to play against the Silver Bullets, the first high profile professional women's baseball team since the All-American Girls Professional League disbanded in 1954.

The Silver Bullets were owned by Hope Beckham, Inc., based in Atlanta, Georgia. In the 1980s, Bob Hope, a former executive with the Atlanta Braves, had tried to establish a minor league women's team, but Minor League Baseball denied his request.

In 1993, the Coors Brewing Company invested $2 million to support the Silver Bullets as they traveled across the country to compete against men's teams, with each player receiving approximately $20,000 per year.

Phil Niekro, a future Hall-of-Famer renowned for his knuckleball, was appointed to manage the team. His pitching style often confused both batters and catchers. Throughout his career, from 1964 to 1987, he became the only knuckleball pitcher to win over 300 games, was selected as an All-Star five times, and led the National League in wins twice. He notably pitched a no-hitter on August 5, 1973.

Upon arriving at the park for pre-game warm-ups, I had the opportunity to speak with Niekro. I thanked him for managing the Silver Bullets and bringing the team to San Antonio.

He replied, "One reason we came is that you built a great stadium. It's been wonderful being with the girls. They are very talented; they just lack the strength of men."

Curious, I asked, "Have you taught them how to throw your knuckleball?"

He explained, "Oh, no. It's a challenging pitch to master. It took me years to learn. You have to dig your fingernails into the ball or use your knuckles for the proper release. There is very little spin, which causes the ball to flutter and dance unpredictably. It's difficult to control and hard to hit. I can also throw a curveball with it."

I noted, "Your brother was quite skilled with the knuckleball too."

He responded, "While my knuckleball was my primary pitch, my brother Joe could throw a fastball and change-up and occasionally used the knuckleball as well."

Phil's brother Joe played in the majors from 1967 to 1988, securing 221 wins and earning a spot as an All-Star. He was also the National League wins leader in 1979.

Former major leaguer Bob Bruce took the mound for us. As he warmed up, I ran out to right field. Suddenly the first batter, a right-handed hitter, hit a high fly ball soaring toward me. Anticipating that the ball would drift toward the sidelines, I sprang into action at the crack of the bat and made a surprising catch.

Later, it was my turn to face hard-throwing sidearm pitcher Venturi. I managed only a weak grounder to third base, which led to an easy out.

After our victory, 6-3, in front of a crowd of 3,000, I spoke with catcher Elizabeth Burnham. I complimented her, saying, "I thought you all played very well."

She replied, "We just started playing two months ago. We have a long way to go to develop into a team that can beat men."

I acknowledged, "We have the advantage of strength, which is not easy to overcome."

With confidence, she responded, "We will see."

I also met Kim Braatz, a four-time All-American college basketball player who would become the first player to hit a home run for the team. Additionally, I spoke with pitcher Pam

Davis and first baseman Julie Croteau, who would make history as the first female players to sign with men's Class A and AA Winter Ball in Hawaii.

The Silver Bullets played from 1994 to 1997, traveling across the country to compete against men's teams. Their demise came when Coors Brewing Company withdrew its sponsorship. Today, the Silver Bullets are honored in the Hall of Fame.

Women have played a significant role in popularizing softball. The game evolved from the original version created by George Hancock, a reporter for the Chicago Board of Trade, on Thanksgiving Day, November 24, 1887—41 years after the Knickerbockers played their first recorded game in Hoboken's Elysian Fields.

The game originated at the Farragut Boat Club in Chicago, following a Harvard-Yale football game. Excited by the announced score, Hancock yelled, "Play ball!" after someone shaped a boxing glove into a ball. Early players even used broomsticks as bats.

The following week, Hancock designed a 17-inch softball, an appropriately sized bat, and a smaller diamond. The game was known by various names, including "kitten ball," "pumpkin ball," and "mush ball."

Initially played indoors, the game moved outdoors in 1888, and Hancock published the first set of official rules in 1889. Unlike baseball, where bases are 90 feet apart, softball bases are only 60 feet apart. The pitcher delivers the ball underhand from a flat surface and from a much closer distance than in hardball.

Eight years after its inception, the first women's softball team was established at Chicago West Division High School in 1895. By 1900, Spalding Sports magazine had dedicated a significant section to women's softball.

It took a long time, because many girls in elementary school did not have the opportunity to play competitive softball. There were exceptions. My stepdaughter Rochelle Hunt played first base in the CYO (Catholic Youth Organization). My granddaughters Sydney played softball for Key Stone elementary school, a highly rated private school.

While I played Little League baseball in 1953, it wasn't until 21 years later that Little League began offering girls the chance to play. In 1974, following a court decision, Little League was required to admit girls, leading to the establishment of a girls' softball division and a softball World Series.

My friend and former Bexar County Commissioner, Trish DeBerry, who I served alongside, began playing in the Perrin Beitel Little League softball in 1975. She was fortunate that the law changed just in time for her to participate.

During lunch one day, she shared, "It was the best time of my life. As a pitcher, I found beauty and grace in the arc of the ball as it left my hand and landed in the catcher's mitt, and the umpire called, 'strike.'"

I asked, "Were you a pretty good player?"

She replied, "I made the All-Stars both years that I played."

Curious, I asked, "Did you get to go to any regional or state finals?"

She responded, "Yes. One year. I thought I wouldn't make it because of my brother's wedding. But my coach called my mom and said he needed me. My mom looked at me and said, 'I guess he needs you to win.' She let me go, and I drove in the winning run. We advanced to the state finals but lost in a very close game."

I said, "I thought playing Little League helped prepare me for the challenges of life. How about you?"

She stated, "The game taught me about sacrifice, team-work, and how to compete and win."

I replied, "Now I understand why you excelled as County Commissioner."

At a chamber music function, I had the opportunity to speak with Peggy Eighmy about Trish's experience with Little League Baseball. To my surprise, Peggy also played, but her experience was quite different from Trish's.

She recalled, "It was a joyous day in 1974 when the *Cambridge Chronicle* reported that girls could now play in Little League. I tried out for the West Cambridge Little League and received a glorious call from Coach Ciampa, informing me that I had been chosen for his team, Armando's Giants."

I asked, "Was the team in the girls' softball division?"

She replied, "No. I played with the boys, just like I used to with my five brothers and their friends on our neighborhood streets. I was always jealous that they got to play Little League Baseball while I did not, even though I was better than several of them."

I inquired, "How were you accepted?"

She answered, "I was one of only two girls in the league, but I never felt less important than the boys. My coach probably protected me from cranky dads."

I asked, "What position did you play?"

She responded, "I played second base. I was a pretty good fielder and a decent hitter."

I continued, "How long did you play?"

She replied, "I played for two years. In my second year, we were league champions. I was devastated when I aged out at 12 years old."

I asked, "Was that experience meaningful to you?"

She said, "I loved my green pinstripe uniform and enjoyed every minute of Little League. I still have my maroon windbreaker that was given to me at our banquet. It has WCLLB embroidered on the front and my name on the right shoulder.

"Now, fifty years later, I reflect on that time with deep affection. Baseball instilled in me a sense of confidence and joy. I cherish the memory of that confident little girl and feel immense gratitude."

Peggy graduated from the University of Massachusetts at Amherst and then embarked on a career in child welfare. She later became the Director of the Massachusetts Attorney General's Consumer Information Service and eventually the President of the University of New Hampshire Foundation. Eight years ago, she relocated to San Antonio when her husband, Taylor, was appointed President of the University of Texas at San Antonio.

Driven by her passion for helping children, Peggy initiated a countywide program for students who have experienced foster care. She collaborated with my wife, Tracy, who worked alongside two judges to establish the Bexar County Children's Court. The State of Texas provided funding, and Peggy successfully raised additional funds, resulting in a 72% increase in the enrollment of students with a history of foster care at UTSA, Texas A&M San Antonio, and the Alamo Colleges.

Simultaneously, Peggy supported her husband, Taylor, in advancing UTSA. In 2024, the University of Texas Board of Regents approved the merger of UTSA with UT Health San Antonio, appointing Eighmy to lead both institutions. This merger brings together 16,000 employees and 40,000 students.

Throughout the years, as chairman of the Bexar County Commissioners, I had the honor of working with Eighmy and Athletic Director Lisa Campos on several UTSA sports projects. Bexar County contributed $25 million toward UTSA sports facilities.

I currently lecture in the UTSA Honors College, which is directed by Vice Provost Jill Fleuriet, as well as for Dr. Lynne Cossman, Dean of the College of Health, Community and Policy.

* * *

The evolution of women's fast-pitch softball began in the 1990s, requiring advanced baseball skills. The underhand pitch can reach speeds of 70 mph from a distance of 43 feet, in contrast to the 60 feet, 6 inches in hardball. This shorter distance complicates hitting, while the reduced base paths demand quick reactions from infielders when fielding grounders. Today, over 600 NCAA member colleges sponsor women's fast-pitch softball programs, with championships held in Divisions I, II, and III.

Locally, the University of the Incarnate Word has a Division II fast-pitch softball team, where Burl Yarbrough's daughter, Alex, played outfield. She now serves as the senior sales manager for the Missions.

On April 4, 2025, I attended a St. Mary's University women's fastpitch softball game with my friend Jenna Saucedo-Herrera, who is president and CEO of Greater:SATX, the economic development public-private agency for the San Antonio region. The St. Mary's university team competes at the NCAA Division II level and has consistently maintained winning records over the past few decades, including a national championship.

During the game, I asked Jenna about her playing days for St. Mary's.

She said, "I played second base from 2006-2009. I was a contact hitter, quick-witted baserunner and usually batted fifth in the lineup. In my junior year while tagging out a player in a vicious rundown between first and second base, I sustained what should have been a career ending elbow injury that required radial head replacement surgery. Instead of quitting, I endured the grueling rehab and played my senior year, but my batting average fell from .361 to .256.

I am who I am because of softball. Playing at the collegiate level changed the trajectory of my life. As captain of the team, I learned that with discipline, hard work, the right attitude and a team to support, you could conquer anything. As a player, I learned how to work my way through the hard knocks of life. Real life, not just the four years of softball eligibility."

At the game Jenna introduced me to her coach, Donna Fields who had retired in July 2024.

I said, "What a remarkable career of 27 years, winning 1076 games, 18 conference titles, four NCAA Regional titles, and the 2002 National Championship, including being in the NCAA Hall of Fame "

She replied, "You seem to know more about me than I do!"

"I followed your career," I said.

After the game St. Mary's President Winston Erevelles recognized Donna for her outstanding career.

I also had the chance to visit with Charlie Migl who had been an assistant coach under Elmer Kosub when we built the baseball stadium in 1968. He went on to be head baseball coach for 35 years. He is the winningest coach in St. Mary's history, winning six conference titles and two national championships. The American Baseball Coaches Association inducted him into the Hall of Fame in January 2025.

He said to me, "Donna and I had a close working relationship during our overlapping careers. It was a longtime friendship, but now when looking back it seems very short."

It was an exciting day to be with Jenna and two baseball legends.

In 2008 during my term as County Judge, we provided $6 million in funding to assist in building the new baseball, softball and soccer facilities. Donna and Charlie led the effort to complete the projects.

The UTSA women's fast pitch softball began in 1992 when they played in the Southland conference. They won three regular season conference titles from 2004-2006, and two NCAA tournaments in 2005 and 2006.

In 2023, when UTSA joined the American Athletic Conference, Director Lisa Campos hired former Mississippi State Coach Vann Stuedeman. She had led the Lady Bulldogs to seven NCAA tournament appearances.

*　*　*

In Division I, eight teams compete in the double-elimination Women's College World Series, which began in Omaha, Nebraska, in 1982. After relocating to California, the series has been hosted in Oklahoma City since 1990, in a stadium that accommodates 13,000 spectators.

During the series, attendance often exceeds 21,000 fans. The excitement of the tournament was particularly evident in 2022, when the final garnered a television rating surpassing that of the men's College World Series. Each year, the event continues to break records for both attendance and viewership.

In 2023, the Women's Professional Fast Pitch League was established, organizing four teams with its headquarters also located in Oklahoma City.

Across the United States, over 25 million men and women participate in recreational softball. Players engage in slow-pitch leagues comprised of men's, women's, and co-ed teams, often formed by employees from various companies or sponsored by businesses.

My son, former Bexar County Commissioner Kevin Wolff, is an accomplished softball player who manages both a competitive men's team and a co-ed team, on which his wife, Sandi, played.

When I asked Sandi about her playing days, she said, "I was a pretty good player because I had played hardball in 1996. We had four teams of girls in the league, playing on the big field during very hot summer days. Unfortunately, 'The League of Our Own' only lasted that one summer. So, when I played softball, the game was easy."

Every Thanksgiving the Wolff Family has a co-ed softball game. Everyone gets to play from 5 to 85 years old, from granddaughter Madeline—the youngest Wolff—to the oldest Wolff, me. We divide up into two teams and play a competitive seven inning games. It's a grand time for the whole family.

On December 3, 2022, just three weeks before my retirement after 22 years as County Judge, county employees honored me with a co-ed softball game at Wolff Stadium. The event was aptly titled "Wolff's Last Inning."

Wearing special red and blue shirts and hats, we divided into two teams of 20 players each. Although my team lost 24 to 18, we had a wonderful time, making it a memorable send-off.

I want to thank George Hancock for the enjoyment we all experienced playing recreational softball and for laying the foundation for the evolution of women's fast-pitch softball. Unfortunately, he has received very little recognition for his pioneering contributions, and I could not find any information about his later life, including his date of death.

George Hancock's invention and development of softball have opened doors for thousands of collegiate women in fast-pitch and recreational softball. We owe him a significant debt of gratitude for expanding opportunities for women in the sport.

Pepper Paire Davis, all-star catcher who played
in the All-American Girls Professional League.

Right: The author with Donna Fields and Jenna Saucedo-Herrera.

Below: The new softball stadium at St. Mary's University.

11. FOR THE LOVE OF THE GAME

IN THE YEAR 2014, with the sun setting on a scorching day in the scrub brush country of South Texas, Tracy and I approached the stunning two-story, 32,000-square-foot white stucco hacienda along the banks of Santa Gertrudis Creek, nestled in the heart of the sprawling King Ranch.

The architecture blended Moorish, Mexican, and California Mission styles, featuring crenelations, corbels, archways, wide verandas, and a tower, while peacocks roamed freely around us.

We were about to enter the headquarters of the illustrious King Ranch for dinner with Tio and Janell Kleberg, the only members of the Kleberg family who live on the ranch.

Once the largest ranch in the world, it still spans 815,000 acres.

The ranch's history began in May 1847 when Richard King arrived in Texas, settling in the Wild Horse Desert, the area between the Nueces and Rio Grande Rivers. In 1853, he purchased his first tract of land, and two years later, on April 14, 1855, he married Henrietta Chambers.

In 1884, King appointed Robert Kleberg Sr. to oversee the ranch's operations. The following year, Kleberg married Richard and Henrietta King's daughter, Alice. After King passed away in 1885 at the Menger Hotel in San Antonio, Robert Kleberg Sr. took charge of the ranch. Following Henrietta's passing, he and Alice became its owners. Kleberg expanded the ranch to over one million acres, building the grand ranch house in 1912, where we would later have dinner.

Over the years, the Kleberg family continued to own and manage the ranch. Stephen J. "Tio" Kleberg was the last family member to oversee operations, managing it from 1979 to 1998. This marked the conclusion of an impressive 114-year history across five generations, establishing a legacy unmatched in ranching and conservation.

During dinner, Tio shared, "Richard King lived during the great cowboy era when land was unfenced, and cattle drives to Kansas were common. In the late 1880s, settlers began to fence the range, the iron horse arrived in town, and then oil was discovered.

I cherished the years I spent running the ranch, continuing a great tradition. I take pride in preserving our land for future generations, balancing cattle raising with the conservation of nature and wildlife."

After dinner, we lingered in the vaulted-ceiling living room, where a painting of the Alamo hung above a large fireplace. On the opposite wall, portraits of Richard King and Henrietta hung side by side.

The next day, Beto Maldonado, author of a book about his experiences as a ranch foreman, took me for a ride in his old red Ford pickup truck. We traveled along some of the 600 miles of gravel roads, passing mesquite, live oak, Shumard, and bur oak trees, some towering as high as 60 feet.

As we drove, we spotted some of the ranch's 35,000 cattle grazing on expansive meadows of blue-stem grass. Surrounded by stunning trees and plants, these meadows rivaled the beauty of any Elysian Fields.

Three years after our visit, in 2017, Donavan Lopez published a book titled *Practice, Practice, Practice,* which recounts the story of the King Ranch Cowboys Baseball team.

After Janell informed Tracy about the book, I called Tio and asked, "Can you tell me about the King Ranch and baseball?"

He replied, "It started in the 1950s when my grandfather Richard Kleberg Sr. believed that the *Vaqueros* who worked our ranch would appreciate the chance to play ball."

Vaqueros are Hispanic cowboys of the Southwest, known for their exceptional horsemanship and roping skills. They spent most of their days in the saddle, herding and branding cattle during the long hours of spring roundups.

Tio continued, "My grandfather built a stadium that seated 400 fans and named it after Assault, our horse who won the Triple Crown of racing in 1946. The ballfield was situated in open spaces among lush green pastures. Before fences were added, outfielders sometimes faced challenges with cows wandering into their paths while chasing down fly balls.

I played right field for our team in 1960 and '61, I knew all the players well, having worked alongside them every day. We shared a common language, and they were my friends.

After long days in the sun, we practiced and prepared for our weekend games, facing teams from across South Texas, including the Red Sox from Refugio, the Braves from Benavides, and the Mohawks from Victoria. Our team was strong, and we had an incredible time together."

I mentioned, "Many Hispanics have proven to be excellent ballplayers. Over 285 major league players are Hispanic." Tio replied, "We had some good ones."

I continued, "While you were playing for the King Ranch team, I was also playing in the Spanish American League in San Antonio. It's possible we crossed paths, as I played against

Victoria and other teams from South Texas."

Tio said, "We may have. We played all over South Texas. Baseball was a great tradition at the ranch. I'm glad Donavan Lopez wrote his book. I'll get you a copy."

While Tio was playing ball in South Texas in 1961, I was playing in San Antonio for the Prospect Hill Yellow Jackets in the Spanish American League. Most of the players were Hispanic and quite skilled. I pitched for the team.

One day, as we stood around at practice, one of the guys mentioned the recently concluded 1960 World Series between the New York Yankees and the Pittsburgh Pirates. Bill Mazeroski hit a walk-off homer in the ninth inning of Game 7 against the Yankees, making it the only walk-off home run to clinch a World Series championship.

The conversation then shifted to Roberto Clemente, who had started playing for the Pirates in 1955 and was an All-Star in 1960 in the year we were playing. He was a source of pride for Hispanic players, inspiring them to play ball. Many of the players predicted he would become one of the greatest players of all time, and they were right. Clemente would go on to be a 15-time All-Star, a two-time World Series Champion, the MVP in 1961, a four-time NL batting champion, and ultimately a Hall-of-Famer.

Many years later, I spoke with my friend Ed Banos, president of the University Health System, who shared a poignant memory of his father, Les, a photographer for the Pittsburgh Pirates.

Ed recounted, "My father was friends with Clemente and had planned to fly with him to Nicaragua in 1972 to help earthquake victims. Fortunately for dad, he was delayed due to work commitments with the Pittsburgh Steelers. Tragically, Clemente died in a plane crash on December 31 at the age of 38."

I had a solid year pitching for the Prospect Hill Yellow Jackets and was drafted by the league champion Centeno Grocery Store to compete for the state title. Unfortunately, I was removed from the team before I even pitched a game because I had played in a doubleheader for my team, Prospect Hill, in Victoria, violating a league rule. That year was the end of playing days for the next 33 years.

I mentioned earlier that the movie *Bull Durham* inspired cities to build new minor league parks, including the one we built. As we were building the park I was persuaded to play ball again.

So, at the age of 53, I stepped out of my car into the damp, cold night at O.P. Schnabel Park, located off Bandera Road. The January 1993 chill seeped through my skin, making me question why I had left the comfort of my living room couch to join a hardball league. This game was not easy for an older man.

I slipped on my warm-up jacket, grabbed my new bat bag filled with my glove, shoes, balls, towels, and bat, and began walking toward the field.

The baseball field is situated in the center of the 200-acre city park on the northwest side of San Antonio. With its large trees, green grass, shrubs, jogging paths, and pavilions, the park resembles the Elysian Fields of Hoboken.

In winter, however, leafless trees with long branches sway above the faded green plywood outfield fence to the music of the wind. Antiquated light poles scattered around cast dim patches of light onto the field.

From the Schnabel Field parking lot, my teammates looked like young boys tossing a ball back and forth on the sidelines. But as I approached, I knew those boyish looks would soon fade away.

I smiled at the memory of my conversation with my

daughter Lynn Slaughter and my granddaughter Hazel Lorenzen about me playing ball again.

Lynn said, "You are going to hurt yourself. Be careful on hot days."

Hazel asked me quizzically, "I thought boys played that game?"

They were both right—I did incur several injuries—like when I slid into home plate and cut my jaw. Boys do play baseball!

Even though we are older, there is a boy trapped in our bodies tugging at our shirt tails, pleading with us to play the game again. Too often we dismiss the urge, claiming we are too old to participate. While our reasoning may be accurate biologically, it is not spiritually valid.

On the sidelines, I tossed the 108-raised red cotton-stitched ball to one of my teammates. Playing catch is a cherished ritual shared between fathers and sons. I could easily envision my dad catching the ball and throwing it back to me, the string of the baseball symbolizing our lifelong connection. Award-winning journalist Bob Costas once suggested that this bond begins when a father rolls a ball across the floor to his infant son.

My teammates came in various shapes and sizes, from plodding, overweight sluggers reminiscent of Paul Bunyan to tall, wiry pitchers, as well as quick little glove men and skilled poke hitters. Despite our differing physiques, there was a place for all of us at the baseball table.

I took the field to shag outfield flies. My reaction time and speed had declined, but I still managed to snag a few under the dim lights. I noticed a small, agile player at shortstop who moved with impressive quickness. When I threw the ball to him, it lacked the velocity I once had in my youth.

Manager Skip Bradley called us in for infield practice. I jogged over to second base, a small area that felt like my own. I paced around my territory, kicking the sand and smoothing it out with my spikes. This was my area to defend, and I relished that responsibility.

By the time Skip was ready to hit, I settled into my obligatory squat position, shifting from my heels to my toes. As the ball approached, I sprang to my right, aiming to trap the erratically bouncing object. The speed of the ball skidded over the infield grass, hopped over hard, uneven patches of red-clumped sand, and sailed right between my legs.

After 30 minutes of infield practice, I could feel the effects of another year on my aging body. The sudden starts and stops put stress on my muscles, tendons, and ligaments.

At our age, the strain on our joints and bones is significant. On a cold winter night like this, it was particularly challenging to keep our muscles warm enough for a necessary burst of speed or a sudden halt. Too often, reaching out to field a ground ball felt like trying to grab a brass ring—almost within reach but always just out of grasp.

After fielding practice, we played a game called "four men up," which allowed six outs before rotating groups. None of us were hitting well; most swung hard but either missed, tipped, fouled, or occasionally made contact.

It was early in the season. Our timing was off, our bodies were out of shape, and sadly, our reaction times had slowed; our eyesight had diminished, and our muscles felt weaker.

As I walked back to my car after the two-hour practice, I began to wonder if I could play without embarrassing myself. In my younger days, I understood the significance of the game, as it taught me the hard lessons of life. But now, I questioned its purpose.

Yet I still enjoyed the smell of freshly cut grass in the out-field, the feel of my cleats striking the hard infield sand, the scent of linseed oil on my glove, the slickness of caulk on my sweaty hands, and the lively sounds of baseball banter. These moments provided an escape from the pressures of the mayor's office.

Being in an all-male environment allowed me to as-sert my masculinity. There are few spaces where men can truly be themselves—a place to spit, scratch freely, bond, share tall tales, joke around, and most importantly, compete against one another.

We were reliving the spirit of the Knickerbockers, a time when baseball was played out of love by amateurs. I be-gan to feel like Frank Pidgeon, who played on the idyllic fields of Hoboken more than 150 years ago. As Pidgeon said, we would "...go out into the green fields, don our ball suits, and go at it with a perfect rush."

In those moments, we felt like boys again. This experi-ence marked my return to the field.

It reminded me of my days as a batboy for the Texas Consolidated semi-pro team 40 years ago. Now, I found myself among the veterans, though I was no longer as skilled.

I also recognized that baseball would offer my aging body a much-needed workout. While it wouldn't restore my former strength, it would help strengthen my muscles, improve my circulatory system, and enhance my sensory perception and coordination.

Baseball embodies timeless grace and beauty, ideally played by athletic bodies that are vibrant, fluid, powerful, and fast. Although our midsections have thickened, our reaction times have slowed, and our hairlines have receded, we can still bring a unique kind of grace to the game. We remain capable of demonstrating balance, dexterity, and agility—like a slow-motion film.

As we practiced throughout January and February, I eagerly awaited the first day of spring on the vernal equinox, when day and night are equal. As the earth warmed, nature rejuvenated us, heralding the start of baseball season.

We became one with the environment, enjoying the soft breeze, the warmth of the sun, the scent of fresh grass, and the sound of chirping birds while playing in our green sanctuary between the white foul lines of play.

On an early spring night in March, we played our first game at St. Mary's University's stadium, which I had helped build 25 years earlier to revive the San Antonio Missions. That night, we looked sharp in blue-striped pants, red caps, and blue mesh shirts, with the red letters "Rangers" emblazoned across our chests.

At our age, dressing like we did in our youth felt almost surreal. But if you're going to play baseball, you should at least look the part. If Kevin Costner had seen us, he might have cast us in one of his baseball films.

Not only did we look good, but we also played well. Skip Bradley pitched five strong innings, allowing only four runs—two of which were unearned. He faced some trouble in the eighth inning, chose to take himself out, and brought in MSBL Commissioner Steve Sigler, who had attended our opening game. Sigler struggled initially but then managed to pitch effectively. We won the game.

After the game, I asked Sigler, "How did you get MSBL started?"

He replied, "In 1987, I placed an ad in a local Long Island paper inviting men aged 30 and older to call me if they wanted to play. I received enough responses to form four teams. Later, I contacted Tom Hayden, who was playing in a West Coast league, and challenged him to a game. Tom accepted, and we held the first bicoastal game."

Hayden was an antiwar activist who later served in the California State Assembly and Senate. He was also married to actress Jane Fonda for 17 years.

I asked, "And where did that lead?"

He responded, "After our game, I sensed an opportunity to create a nationwide league. I began establishing affiliates across the country.

I reached out to sports editors nationwide, encouraging them to write about our new league. On July 4, 1988, Sports Illustrated published a story, and we received stacks of mail from eager players across the country wanting to join.

That same year, the film *Bull Durham* was released, which had an inspirational impact on me and thousands of other adult men."

I asked, "When did you hold the first World Series?"

He replied, "Our first full season was in 1988, and we held our inaugural MSBL World Series that October in Phoenix, Arizona. Thirty-eight teams and 500 players showed up to play. We were off and running."

I said, "We all owe you a big thanks."

In addition to the Men's Senior Baseball League, the Roy Hobbs League, based in Akron, Ohio, and the National Adult Baseball Association (NABA), based in Denver, Colorado, were established. Together, these three leagues engage approximately 100,000 male participants.

In addition to these national leagues, there are hundreds of regional sandlot leagues. While the three national leagues are organized and managed by paid staff, sandlot baseball operates in a loose and less expensive manner.

In 2023, I threw the first pitch for a newly created sandlot

THE ELYSIAN FIELDS *of* BASEBALL

team at Pittman Sullivan Field on the east side of San Antonio.

A year later, I met Josh Huskins, a self-employed photographer, who said, "I remember when you threw out the first pitch for our newly formed sandlot league last year."

I asked, "Are you still playing?"

He replied, "We're in our second year and have six teams, including the Roses, which is the team I play for. The other teams are the Dingers, Slowpokes, Tigers, War Hawks, and Los Morones."

We play about 12 games each season, plus a few matchups against other sandlot teams in Austin and Houston. It's the players' responsibility to organize and manage their teams, including seeking sponsorships to cover expenses like uniforms, umpires, and field rentals. If fundraising falls short, we contribute $20 per game as needed. Food trucks are available at our games, and there are no age restrictions, though players typically range from 16 to 45 years old. We do not crown a league champion.

All participants are volunteers. Occasionally, we generate some revenue during our games at Wolff Stadium, which we typically donate to a toy drive for children. The league operates democratically.

While the movie *Bull Durham* inspired older men to return to play ball, I believe films like *The Natural* and *Field of Dreams* have also profoundly rekindled older men's love for the game.

The Natural, produced by and starring Robert Redford in 1988, is based on Bernard Malamud's 1951 novel. In the film, a young boy named Roy Hobbs carves a magical bat from a tree, naming it "Wonder Boy," reminiscent of King Arthur's sword Excalibur.

After years away from baseball, Hobbs returns to play for the Knights, a fictional team symbolizing the knights of King

Arthur's court. The Knights win the pennant—referred to as the Holy Grail—when the aging rookie Hobbs hits a game-winning home run in the final inning. This supernatural moment unfolds as the ball strikes the lights, causing them to crackle and pop like fireworks as Hobbs rounds the bases.

We can all imagine ourselves hitting a home run like the old man Hobbs. His legacy is so impactful that an amateur national league was named in his honor. The Roy Hobbs Baseball League now boasts 750 teams and 10,000 players.

Kevin Costner's *Field of Dreams*, released in 1989 is based on W. P. Kinsella's 1982 novel *Shoeless Joe Jackson*. I own a first edition of Kinsella's book, which is part of my collection of 250 first edition baseball titles.

In the movie, Ray Kinsella walks through his cornfield one evening and hears a voice whisper, "If you build it, he will come." Prompted by this voice, Kinsella constructs a baseball field in the cornfield.

"Shoeless" Joe Jackson and his teammates emerge from the corn to play against other legendary players, including Gil Hodges and Mel Ott.

Kinsella's deceased father appears in a catcher's uniform. When Ray asks him, "Is there a heaven?" his father replies, "Yes, it is a place where dreams come true."

The ghosts of baseball's past, along with Kinsella's father, invoke the power of baseball's tradition of metaphysics and supernatural beliefs that rival any religion. Perhaps one day, I will have the chance to play another game of catch with my father.

Field of Dreams was filmed on a farm in Dubuque County, Iowa, where Major League Baseball held a game on August 12, 2021. The White Sox, the team Shoeless Joe Jackson played for, defeated the Yankees 9-8. This event attracted more television viewers than any regular-season game in 16 years.

Each year, over 100,000 people visit the Field of Dreams. Some choose to get married at home plate, while others spread the ashes of loved ones or seek paranormal experiences.

A month after our first game at St. Mary's Field, I crouched in right field at Rosedale Park, ready for the crack of the bat to send a baseball my way. Instead, I heard gunfire behind me. I turned to see kids on the neighboring soccer and T-ball fields hitting the ground while others ran down the street.

Police Chief Bill Gibson had warned me to be cautious due to death threats I received. I had dismissed it at the time, but the sound of gunshots made me realize the seriousness of the situation.

The police arrived promptly to assist my security team in searching the area. We soon discovered that the shots had been fired from a nearby street during a drive-by shooting involving a youth gang. Thankfully, no one was hurt, and we resumed the game as if nothing had happened.

A few days later, I met with several members of the youth gangs. They explained that they had joined these groups due to broken homes, seeking the sense of family that the gangs provided.

I believed that expanding baseball and other sports opportunities could help many young boys gain a sense of family. This conviction led to the creation of "The Coalition," a public-private initiative aimed at providing a supportive environment for these boys.

We enrolled over 30,000 kids in our programs, many of whom took part in baseball. Several players from our league generously volunteered their time, and the Missions provided free tickets to their games. Through baseball, the kids developed a sense of direction and discipline. I successfully advocated for a $10 million increase in our city budget for recreational programs.

As the season unfolded, we reveled in the joy of playing out our dreams and fantasies. Our senses were awakened: the feel of the bat and glove, the sight of a perfectly executed play, the smell of rosin, leather, and sweat, the sound of a well-hit line drive, and the sweet taste of victory.

Our bodies reconnected with nature, and just as nature heals itself, it healed us. We longed for the freedom to run and compete, allowing us to test our skills. Neither age nor life's challenges could diminish our vitality.

We got to know our teammates better, and the bonds we formed grew stronger as we supported one another in healing our bodies, minds, and souls—just as our baseball ancestors had done for over a century.

Throughout the season, I developed a camaraderie with my teammates. We shared jokes, played pranks, cheered each other on, and assisted with any problems a teammate faced. These relationships fostered strength and confidence; they were the human glue that bound us together.

The players' skills progressed from poor to good, but regardless of skill level, everyone had a role on a team. Many of the skilled players I encountered had transitioned from professional baseball.

In one memorable game, I faced former Major League pitcher Bob Bruce, who made his debut with the Detroit Tigers in 1959—the same year I graduated from high school. Bruce had a nine-year career in the majors, playing in 219 games with an ERA of 3.85 and achieving 49 wins.

Bruce graciously threw only fastballs but proved to be challenging to hit. He delivered a two-seam fastball that sank slightly, followed by a four-seam fastball that had a rise. His pitches were expertly placed on the edges of the plate. Although I made contact, I often hit the ball with either the end of the bat or near my hands, resulting in pop-ups or ground balls.

After the game, I spoke with him and learned that he began playing in the MSBL at age 57. He shared, "I look forward to every MSBL game as much as I did to a Major League game. The competitiveness rekindled my spirit. My teammates made a difference in my life."

Like Bruce, baseball's spirit profoundly impacted thousands of men who returned to the playing fields, leading to extraordinary moments.

Our league also included a professional basketball player and coach: Doug Moe, who coached the San Antonio Spurs from 1976 to 1980. In 1994, at age 56, Doug began playing senior league baseball. One day before a game, we had a conversation.

Doug reflected, "I enjoyed my years in basketball, but I've always loved baseball. I believe that if we hadn't lost our green fields during my childhood, I would have become a professional baseball player instead of a basketball player."

I replied, "Well, you do have a very smooth swing."

He responded, "As a kid, I used to switch-hit. After I had a knee replacement on my left knee, I decided to bat left-handed to relieve pressure on my right knee."

I commented, "You really hit the ball deep."

He explained, "I favor Ted Williams' approach to hitting. I swing with a slight uppercut. If I can get the ball in the air and hit it deep, the outfielders struggle to chase it down because they lack the speed. I'm so thankful to finally be playing the game I love again."

Years later, when Doug turned 86 in 2024, I asked if he was still following baseball.

He replied, "I watch some of the World Series. I still

can't forgive the Dodgers for leaving Brooklyn. I attended many games there as a kid, paying 60 cents to sit in the bleachers. Duke Snider was my favorite player.

"I still play ball; it's just fantasy baseball now. It's easier on my knees."

On Sunday morning, May 16, 1999, during our fourth game of the season, we faced the 40+ Austin Twins at Southwest Texas State University's Bobcat Stadium in San Marcos. I was 58 years old at the time.

I picked up Roy Hobbs' magical bat, crafted from a tree like King Arthur's sword Excalibur, and walked to the plate. With two outs and a man on first, I found myself facing an 0-2 count. I let the third pitch go by; it was just outside for a ball.

As the next pitch approached, I felt liberated, my mind clear of distractions. I focused solely on the ball, a fastball roaring toward the middle of the plate. I had never seen the ball so clearly before.

In that moment of relaxed confidence, I executed a perfect swing with impressive bat speed, making solid contact right in front of the plate. As I sprinted to first base, a thought crossed my mind: "Could this finally be it?"

I didn't watch the ball, but the roar of my teammates indicated it had cleared the fence. Rounding second base, I saw my teammates emerging from the dugout, ready to give me high fives at third and embraces at home plate. They excitedly informed me that my home run had sailed over the left-center-field wall, approximately 345 feet from home plate. This was the first home run I had hit since returning to baseball five years earlier.

I sensed that something extraordinary had happened, and it was not merely luck. Too many factors had aligned perfectly: the weather, a favorable pitch, and the harmony of my body, mind, and soul.

At home plate, I was met with high fives and laughter. One teammate quipped, "We're sending your bat for analysis," while another joked, "Did the pitcher throw you a 'Do you need a napkin with that pitch?'" Meanwhile, my manager, Skip Bradley, declared, "Yard (home run hitter), I'm moving you up to third in the batting order."

* * *

When I got home, still buzzing with excitement, I said to Tracy, "I hit my first home run because the temperature, barometric pressure, and humidity were all in harmony, and I made a perfect swing."

She replied, "No, that's not the reason. You've never hit a home run before, and you probably won't again. At 58 years old, you were in a different realm, in some mystical zone. The powerful Greek God Zeus blessed you."

I countered, "Well, Thomas Moore did say that we need gods and myths to give us spirituality and free us from our human confines. So, you might be right; Zeus granted me that one special moment."

Time proved Tracy right; I never hit another home run.

As spring fades, the Northern Hemisphere tilts toward the sun, bringing hotter days. The ancient Greeks began their Olympic games on the summer solstice, the year's longest day, when temperatures soar into the mid to high 90s.

By the time the summer solstice arrives, the longest day of the year, the ball seems to hang in the air, suspended in time. My swing has developed a natural fluidity as I balance on the balls of my feet. On the field, I skillfully control my approach to ground balls and throw with a bit of loft because my straight, level throws often end up in the dirt. When I pitch, I focus on staying within myself, aiming low at specific spots and allowing the batter to do the work.

During summer days, we must blend with nature and protect ourselves from the scorching sun, as our aging hearts and cardiovascular systems endure significant stress in the heat. Although our hearts still beat 100,000 times a day, pumping five quarts of blood through our bodies every minute, this process becomes increasingly challenging with age.

The reduced elasticity of our blood vessels slows down blood flow and decreases circulation to our muscles. Additionally, our bodies lose fluids from sweating.

Rather than ignoring the dangers of the sun and health concerns, we must work with nature to safeguard ourselves. We should pace ourselves and stay hydrated while enjoying the natural world.

We don't have a home field, so we've played on various fields in San Antonio and throughout Texas. Not all the ballparks we visit are nestled in beautiful Elysian Fields.

In May 2000, we played at Galena Ballpark, situated in an industrial suburb known for its numerous refineries. The park was surrounded on three sides by a stagnant, milky-looking reservoir.

The grass was brown, and both the lights and infield were in poor condition. A dirt road and a railroad track ran parallel to the right-field foul line, while passing trucks on the dirt road coated the field in dust.

Upon our arrival, a pleasant breeze greeted us; however, we were unaware that the nearby reservoir was swarming with mosquitoes, lying in wait for the wind to die down and the sun to set.

As the sun began to lower during the second inning, the first wave of mosquitoes launched their attack. Their assault was temporarily halted when a truck on the dirt road sprayed mosquito repellent, killing the pests but leaving us momentarily blinded and forcing a pause in the game.

In the third inning, a second wave of blood-sucking insects overwhelmed us. We found ourselves swatting more mosquitoes than baseballs.

Aside from Galena Park, most of the ballfields we play on are located in parks that offer the joys of trees, grass, shrubs, and wildflowers—elements that inspire us and shield us from the harsh sun.

In San Antonio, the magic and beauty of nature are best exemplified at Incarnate Word University, which is situated in an urban environment on the near north side. The baseball field is insulated from the intense urban surroundings by 50 acres of nature park adjacent to the field, an Elysian Field unmatched.

On those 50 wooded acres, a rock wall encircles a pool of crystal-clear, cool water known as the Blue Hole. This pristine water bubbles up from the underground Edwards Aquifer and serves as the headwaters of the San Antonio River, which I grew up alongside south of the city. Whenever I return for a baseball game at the stadium near the woods, I always seize the opportunity to visit this enchanting natural site.

The most remarkable aspect of this landscape lies beneath our feet. The expansive limestone Karst Edwards Aquifer is one of the most productive artesian aquifers in the world, holding between 25 to 55 million acre-feet of water. It spans 4,350 square miles and reaches approximately 80 miles in width.

After heavy rains, I've sometimes witnessed water bubbling up from the ground on the northern edge of the UIW campus, surrounded by several oak and palm trees. It's a magical sight, as natural springs release clear water from the Edwards Aquifer.

Playing at Incarnate Word also gave me the privilege of meeting Danny Heep, the university's baseball team coach. He played in the Major Leagues from 1979 to 1991 and was part of two World Series championship teams: the New York Mets in 1986 and the Atlanta Braves in 1991.

I remarked, "It's amazing that two players from San Antonio were on Mets championship teams—Grote in 1969 and you in 1986."

He responded, "Jerry Grote caught every game in the 1969 World Series, while I had only one hit and two RBIs in the '86 World Series."

I asked, "But you accumulated over 500 hits and 30 home runs in your career. How did you choose your bats?"

He explained, "I looked for bats with a wide grain. If I could find one with a knot on the sweet spot, I knew that the harder wood would help me drive the ball farther. Only a small portion of the bat can be used to hit the ball solidly, and the sweet spot is about the width of two baseballs."

I inquired, "How many bats did the team provide you?"

He replied, "I was issued 36 bats at the start of each season. I would select the best 12 for games, keep another 12 in reserve for when my main bats broke, and use the remaining 12 for batting practice."

I asked, "Should I stand at the front or the back of the plate?"

He responded, "I preferred to stand at the back of the plate because a Major League hitter has about two-tenths of a second to swing. My good vision and depth perception allowed me to judge the ball's distance, speed, and spin.

In senior ball, it's best to stand at the front because the pitchers' fastballs have considerably slowed down. This position helps against the sinker, knuckleball, and breaking ball.

Keep your front shoulder in; if you open your shoulder too soon, you'll only be able to hit inside pitches."

Another magnificent natural Elysian baseball field stands at the Naaman Forest High School ballpark, adjacent to the botanically sensitive Spring Creek Forest Preserve in Dallas, Texas. The large shade trees and shrubs surrounding the fields create a habitat for singing birds, dragonflies, squirrels, and countless other animals. I played there during the MSBL Texas Cup Tournament over the July 4th weekend in 1999, enduring particularly sweltering heat.

As I stood in right field, waiting for an occasional ball to come my way, I wore sunglasses and kept my cap pulled low to shield myself from the sun. Instead of focusing on the heat, I absorbed the beauty of nature around me. I gazed down at the lush green grass, then up at the towering trees while anxiously pawing at the ground and pounding my glove, awaiting a ball that never arrived.

While waiting to bat, I slipped away to a small hill behind our dugout. I lay beneath a tree, nestled in a bed of wild yellow flowers, as birds chirped, and a gentle breeze cooled me.

I sipped some water and closed my eyes, listening to the players' voices blending with the cicada chorus from the forest: "Come on, Clean Up Charlie," "One down," "Foul ball," "Got them popping up," "Good poke," "Fair ball," "Hustle," and "Home, home, home."

Amid these voices were the familiar sounds of baseball—the crack of the bat against the ball and the ball slamming into the glove.

There is much truth in the 23rd Psalm, which states:

He (God) makes me lie down in green pastures...
He restores my soul.

I felt an immense sense of relaxation as I absorbed the sweetness of nature and the sounds of baseball surrounding me. When the inning concluded, I hopped off the hill and dashed back into the outfield.

As life unfolds, the slow-paced game of baseball offers a chance to nurture the soul while appreciating the beauty of nature.

For those of us traveling to the Elysian fields of Phoenix, Arizona, it's an exhilarating time as we prepare to compete in the MSBL World Series. I will join over 6,800 adult amateur players in the largest amateur baseball tournament in the world. It's remarkable to think that just 500 players participated in the inaugural MSBL World Series, a number that has now increased to over 9,000.

Teams compete in multiple brackets based on age and skill level, with each team scheduled to play six games over four days.

Major League Baseball has six training facilities in the Phoenix area, each equipped with excellent stadiums and several practice fields. Because these facilities are publicly owned, our league has the opportunity to play on these well-manicured fields at the Phoenix World Series. Additionally, we use high school and college fields, as up to 100 teams compete simultaneously.

As October approaches, anticipation builds among the 15 percent of MSBL players heading to the World Series. Many pack their families and food into their cars and head west to enjoy the expansive sky and dry air. We are all off to the Big Show. I played in my first World Series in 1997 in the 50+ division. We arrived on Sunday, the day before the tournament started, and just stepping out into the cool October Arizona weather was enough to elevate our spirits for the upcoming games.

Our first night included a practice session at Tempe Diablo Stadium, a 9,785-seat training facility for the Anaheim Angels and home to their minor-league affiliate, the Tempe Diablos.

This state-of-the-art stadium is set in a scenic area, framed by a picturesque mountain that rises behind the left-field fence. Before our minor-league stadium was constructed in San Antonio in 1994, I visited this venue, among others, to learn and adapt several of its features for our park.

The next day, we split a double-header. While relaxing on the grass before our game, we took in nature and enjoyed watching another match unfold. Between games, we savored a picnic of apples and sandwiches.

On the following day, we again split a double-header. In the second game, played under the lights, I had my best performance of the series. With Sam De Los Santos at shortstop and me at second base, we executed two double plays. I recorded two hits, one of which bounced just shy of the left-field fence.

The next day, we lost another double-header, marking the end of our tournament journey. We finished with a 2-4 record. Nonetheless, it was wonderful to see so many men enjoying themselves and playing this great game. The laughter, camaraderie, and competitive spirit of players from all over the world made the experience truly exciting.

Several former Major League players participated in the World Series. While I was playing second base, I had a conversation with Bert Campaneris after he hit a double. I thanked him for joining us. Bert played shortstop from 1964 to 1983, primarily with the Oakland A's, where he amassed 2,249 hits and achieved a .963 fielding average.

Over the years, I played in three World Series.

Occasionally, Mission Old-Timer games are held at Wolff Stadium, featuring former participants from the minor or major leagues with ties to San Antonio. I was invited to play in one of these games on May 1, 1999, likely because I built the stadium during my tenure as mayor.

Before the game, I spoke with Jerry Grote, who once got a hit off me in the Spanish American League in 1961; it was a Texas Leaguer to left-center field.

Grote was born in San Antonio, attended MacArthur High School, and then Trinity University. He played his first major league season with the Houston Colts in 1963 and his last game with the Los Angeles Dodgers in 1981, although he spent most of his career with the New York Mets from 1966 to 1977.

An exceptional catcher, Grote played one of the most challenging positions in baseball. With each pitch, he squatted with his rear just a few inches off the ground. He would drop to his knees to stop pitches in the dirt or block a runner barreling toward him at home plate. Quick reflexes were essential for throwing out baserunners at second base. A catcher requires a thick neck, strong forearms, a robust back, sturdy legs, quick hands, and a powerful wrist.

I asked Grote to share the story of the magical 1969 Mets season.

He said, "We finished in ninth place the year before, which was only the second time in seven years we had ended that high. In 1969, we lost seven of our first ten games, but we were young and fearless and never gave up. We began to connect with one another and finally started winning. Our fans became energized by our spirit, and we fed off their enthusiasm, accomplishing what was thought to be impossible.

"Although we were still behind the Cubs by 9½ games on August 15, we won the National League pennant. We were heavy underdogs in the World Series. After losing the first game, we went on to win four straight against Baltimore. I caught every inning of the series."

I replied, "That is hard to believe, but you did have a remarkable young pitcher, Tom Seaver, who won 25 games that year and secured a victory in his second World Series start."

He responded, "It was a joy to catch him. He went on to become a Hall-of-Famer."

Though Grote was not known for his hitting, he was celebrated as the best catcher of his generation. A two-time All-Star, he is a member of the New York Mets Hall of Fame.

Grote passed away in 2024.

At 72 years old, Carl Scheib struck out the first batter in our old timers game. Scheib had a patchy career in the major leagues from 1943 to 1954, having started at just 16, making him the youngest player in American League history.

He wore a pair of kangaroo-skin leather shoes, complete with black shoelaces and steel spikes—the same shoes he had on when he walked off the mound for the last time in 1954.

As I glanced at his shoes, I was transported back in time. Rawlings manufactured shoes that had a brilliant shine, reminiscent of how the clubhouse boy would polish Carl's before each game.

In the dugout, I asked him, "How are you able to pitch effectively even now?"

He replied, "I lead with my legs and lower body as I step toward the plate. I keep my body closed and hide the ball by raising my elbow and turning my shoulder to block the pitch from the batter's view."

Carl Scheib passed away in San Antonio on March 24, 2018.

Mike Shull, who played shortstop in the Angels organization, was also present. A large man, he had blown out his arm while pitching, which ended his career; however, he still possessed a powerful throw.

He fielded a grounder and threw it sharply to first base. Lefty Falcon, with his glove extended, let the ball slip past and hit him in the head. Shaking it off, he walked back to the dugout, fortunate to have a hard head.

Back in the dugout, I spoke with Cliff Johnson, who grew up in San Antonio and attended Wheatley High School. He began his major league career in 1972 with the Astros and concluded it with the Toronto Blue Jays in 1986. Over his career, he hit 196 home runs and played on two World Series championship teams.

I asked him, "How close should you stand to the plate?"

He responded, "It depends on how quick you are. I had quick hands, so I stood close to the plate. Being near the plate and using a long bat prevented the pitcher from delivering outside pitches.

With my good bat speed, I could hit pitches in the strike zone. If a pitcher made a mistake and threw it inside, I had the ball exactly where I wanted it."

I further inquired, "Do your muscles really remember?"

He replied, "After hitting every day for years, my muscle memory became locked in. The more you swing, the better your muscles remember. My muscles had a long-term memory, and my batting average improved as I got older. I achieved my best batting average, .304, in 1984 when I was 37 years old. I never settled for weak hits or became a 'Punch and Judy' hitter. If I had a rough night, I didn't dwell on it."

Curious, I asked, "Did you lift weights?"

He responded, "When I started playing, baseball didn't emphasize weightlifting. We were told that baseball is an elastic game requiring a full range of muscle mobility. There were concerns that lifting weights would tighten your chest muscles and limit flexibility, so I avoided it. However, philosophies changed over time. By the time I left baseball, every team had specialists in weight training."

As I stepped up to the plate, Gary Bell stood on the mound, grinning at me. "I'm going to throw you nothing but roundhouse curves. So, get ready," he said.

Cliff's advice was of no help; I struck out swinging. After the game, I asked, "Hey, why didn't you throw me a fastball?"

He replied, "When I played for the Cleveland Indians, I would challenge hitters on the inside to break their bats. After I lost my fastball, I focused on getting movement on the ball and throwing sliders on the outside of the plate. I grip the high seam on the ball for the curve, so that's what you got."

I suggested, "Let's meet up with Horlen for a light lunch."

He responded, "Love to."

Joe Horlen has been Bell's lifelong friend since their days at Luther Burbank High School. Horlen won 116 major league games from 1961 to 1972, with an ERA of 3.11 and 1,065 strikeouts. In 1967, while playing for the Chicago White Sox, he pitched a no-hitter. That year, he went 19-7 and had the lowest ERA in the American League at 2.06.

When Horlen arrived for lunch, I said, "I remember when you pitched for the Missions."

He replied, "I took the mound for them in 1973, one year after finishing my major league career. After that, I played for the St. Lucie Legends in the Senior Professional Baseball Association."

I asked, "What are you doing now?"

He said, "I throw batting practice for San Francisco's Triple-A Fresno Grizzlies. I still have a strong arm because I ran and threw a lot between games throughout my career. I never missed a starting assignment.

"I had to stay in shape because pitching is demanding.

"When I throw a 90-mph fastball, my arm moves downward at about 97 mph. I release the ball from about 55 feet away, and it travels at 132 feet per second.

"My back bends, and my legs take a beating when I land after throwing. My muscles stretch and tear. Pitchers are prone to injuries in their shoulders, elbows, and knees. To endure, you need strong muscles in your thighs and torso."

I asked him if he had any advice on pitching?"

He said, "Work on strengthening your arm by throwing the ball 60 to 70 feet. Always throw strikes. If you get the first pitch over for a strike, the chances of the hitter getting a hit go down by 10 percent. Also, if a hitter is behind in the count, they are more likely to swing at the next pitch, even if it's slightly off the plate. If you walk the leadoff hitter, they will likely score."

Over the years, Horlen, Bell, and I continued to share lunches together. During our last lunch, Horlen spoke only a few words, and we understood why: Alzheimer's had begun to affect him in 2017. Horlen passed away on April 10, 2022, at the age of 84.

However, the good Lord is still watching over Bell, who is now 87 years old.

I played in the Men's Senior League for 16 years, retiring in 2010 when I turned 69. Nevertheless, when I reached 81 in 2021, Skip Bradley convinced me to join his team. I donned a uniform and cap and took to the outfield for the pre-game warm-up.

As I stood there, a dusty darkness enveloped me when a fly ball was hit my way. I raised my glove, but the ball sailed past and struck me on the cheek. During the game, I managed to hit a Texas Leaguer to right field. However, as I sprinted toward first base, I fell, having strained a muscle. Hobbled off the field, I realized exactly why I had retired II years earlier.

We contributed to keeping the amateur game alive, and I like to think that the young men who played baseball for the love of the game on the Elysian Fields of Hoboken in the 1800s would be proud of us. Old men playing amateur hardball will keep the fires burning for the pioneers who introduced us to the game we came to love.

While my playing days came to an end, I enjoyed watching ball games especially when my stepson Paul Wendland's son and my grandson Ben Wendland played. For over ten years, we watched him play Little League all the way to high school. In his final year, 2024, at Alamo Heights High School, he received an all-district honorable mention.

I watch the Little League playoffs. In the 2024 Little League World Series, a team from Boerne, just 20 miles from San Antonio, made it to the American team finals but lost. Unlike the advice I received when I pitch in Little League the pitchers were throwing curves and sliders. Two day's rest was not enough for Boerne's star pitcher to pitch in the final championship game.

I catch all the MLB World Series games. I watched every game of the 2024 World Series between the Yankees and Dodgers which quickly became a nightmare for the Yankees. They lost the first game when Freddie Freeman hit a walk-off grand slam, an incredible achievement that had never previously occurred in that context.

After the Yankees lost the first game, they went on to lose the next two games, and then the Yankees finally won the fourth game.

In the fifth game, they took a commanding 5-0 lead, bolstered by a home run from Aaron Judge, who had faced challenges throughout the series. However, the fifth inning proved

Above: Missions "Old Timers" game at Wolff Stadium. I am standng 11th from left.
Below: MSCB Texans. I am standing far left.

disastrous: Judge dropped a fly ball, shortstop Anthony Volpe made an errant throw to third base, allowing a runner to reach safely, and pitcher Gerrit Cole failed to cover first base. This sequence of errors led to five unearned runs for the Dodgers in that inning, enabling them to win the game and secure the World Series title. A very disappointing series.

Each year I catch the men's college playoffs and the women's fast pitch softball playoffs and still go to some of the Mission's games and a few MLB games in Houston and New York. And as you now know, I wrote this book.

Above: With my brothers Gary (left) and George at our annual Thanksgiving family game.

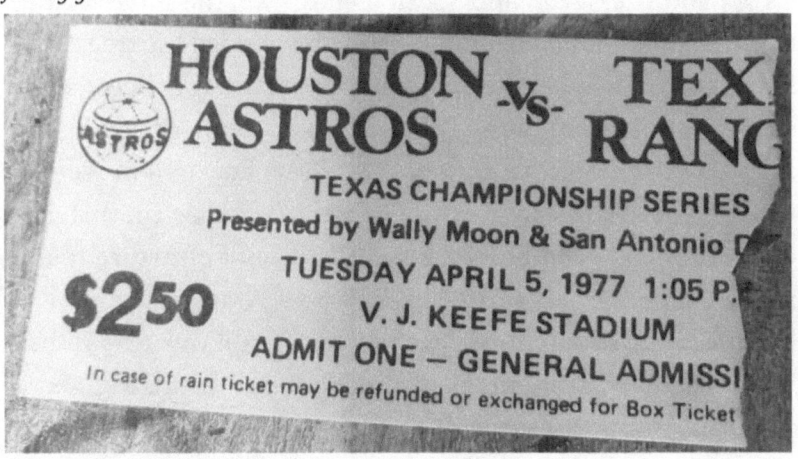

Memories are made of this! Ticket stub from a ball game between the Houston Astros and Texas Rangers at the ballfield we built at St. Mary's. Note the price of admission! (Ticket courtesy Pat Frost)

12. THE PROMISED LAND

THERE EXISTS A WAY to play ball forever in the American Promised Land of Elysian Fields. This paradise is a refuge laden with golden flowers, majestic trees, and meadows reminiscent of the Greek Elysian Fields, where the righteous Greeks resided eternally near the stream of Okeanos, known as the Isles of the Blessed.

The American Promised Land also resembles the terrestrial paradise of the Garden of Eden as described in Genesis 2-3 and Ezekiel 28 and 30. In Genesis 2:8, the Bible tells us that the Lord planted a paradise, which included the tree of the knowledge of good and evil. This sacred space is believed to be situated at the head of the Persian Gulf in southern Mesopotamia, where the Tigris and Euphrates rivers flow into the sea.

The American Promised Land embodies the magical connection between baseball and the beauty of nature found in the Elysian Fields of Hoboken, where America's game was born. The mystique, lore, legends, and traditions of baseball thrive in the vibrant energy of this Promised Land. Righteous players and contributors to the game who have passed discover a unique spirituality that intertwines baseball and nature, creating an eternal haven.

The Promised Land exists here on Earth, akin to *The Bible's* Garden of Eden and the Greek Elysian Fields. While I am uncertain about the activities that await the faithful in the

Garden of Eden and the Greek Elysian Fields, I do know what we will do in the American Promised Land: we will play ball.

Our Promised Land is also located by a river, much like the stream of Okeanos and the Tigris and Euphrates Rivers. This river is not far from the Elysian Fields of Hoboken, nestled between the Adirondack and Catskill mountains in central New York. It is a lush paradise alongside the northern branch of the Susquehanna River, believed to be the oldest river in the world, flowing from its headwaters at Otsego Lake.

Native Americans have inhabited the banks of the Susquehanna River for centuries. Among them, the influential Oneida Nation, one of the five nations of the Iroquois Confederacy, stands out. The name "Oneida," which means "Place of the Rock," refers to a boulder located on Otsego Lake near the Susquehanna River's outlet. The other four nations in the Iroquois Confederacy are the Mohawk, Onondaga, Cayuga, and Seneca.

The Iroquois have a special resting place, a large meadow surrounded by trees next to the river, close to the Susquehanna's headwaters. This land has been set aside to honor their once-mighty presence. But the Iroquois continue to inhabit this space, as expressed in their prayer: "Do not think of me as gone. I am with you still—in each new dawn."

The spirits of the Iroquois are pleased that baseball is played eternally along the banks of the river. Native American baseball players have a long history, dating back to 1887, when Louis Sockalexis played in Major League Baseball for the Cleveland Spiders.

Six years later, from 1903 to 1925, Charles Albert "Chief" Bender achieved an impressive record of 212 wins and 127 losses while pitching for three world championship teams. In one World Series, he pitched three complete games. Bender became the first Native American enshrined in the Hall of Fame. In total, fifty-two Native Americans have played in Major League Baseball, including Olympic medalist Jim Thorpe.

In June 2024, my sons Scott and Matthew, along with Matthew's 10-year-old son Gideon, flew to New York. After renting a car, we journeyed through the Adirondack and Catskill Mountains. I kept an eye out for evidence of the Elysian Fields, eventually arriving at the house Scott had rented near the river. The house is nestled on the edge of a meadow and framed by towering mountains, providing an ideal location for a baseball field.

Late on our first night, I was awakened by the unmistakable crack of a bat. Looking out the window, I could see only hazy clouds drifting low over the meadow. Surely, the sound must have come from an immortal baseball player hitting a ball hard, just like you hear when someone hits a home run.
When I recounted this story to my sons the next morning, they said I had a vivid imagination.

I simply smiled and replied, "We are in a spiritual haven that only those who believe can truly perceive. We are surrounded by the spirits of ballplayers who are still playing the game."

Scott responded, "If you say so."

Matt smiled and added, "I will keep an eye out."

I continued, "You must open your mind to the possibilities of different kinds of heavens."

As we drove along the river and later walked alongside it, I envisioned the game being played as it has been through three centuries. I could see the Magnolia Ball Club, the Gothams, and the Knickerbockers, along with players from the Roy Hobbs Baseball League, the Men's Senior Baseball League, and the National Adult Baseball Association.

Frank Pidgeon and his Knickerbocker teammates were

engaged in a pick-up game against an all-star team from the Men's Senior League. Playing under Knickerbocker rules, they emerged victorious over the All-Stars.

On another field, the women of the All-American Girls Professional Baseball League took to the diamond. Players from the National Women's Hall of Fame, including Jean Faut, Doris Sands, Jean Winter, and Pepper Paire Davis, stepped onto the field, with Davis continuing to catch and drive in runs with her powerful line drives.

Later, the women from the Laurel and Abernakis Baseball Club challenged the Silver Bullets. They put up a good fight but ultimately lost the game to the Bullets.

On yet another field, the Negro Leagues continued their games. Players, including Carl Long, Jimmy Dean, Ira McKnight, and John "Mule" Miles, took the field, enjoying the camaraderie of playing alongside friends.

The Texas Consolidated Transporters are in action, featuring players like Blas Monaco, Texas Jack Kraus, and Alex De La Garza. They recruited my dad, who showcased his signature fastball from his days with the Highland Park team. He pitched a remarkable seven-hitter game and secured the win. One day, I hope to join him, and together we will pitch a triumphant game.

There is also a women's fast-pitch softball league featuring many college stars. On the sidelines, George Hancock watches in amazement as the sport he helped shape has evolved over the years.

Tucked away is the Cathedral of Baseball, reminiscent of Wrigley Field. In this ballpark, some of the 19,500 major league players who have passed on continue to enjoy the game. You can see players like Joe Horlen, Jerry Grote, and Jim Bouton in action, cherishing the sport they love.

Nearby is a chapel akin to Wolff Stadium, where minor

league players revel in their games. The San Antonio Missions, featuring outfielder Collins (1907), outfielder Ike Boone (1923), and pitcher Bob Mucrief (1940), recently triumphed over the Austin Senators.

Overseeing the players and games on the Elysian Fields are the gods of Baseball. They reside in a castle resembling Mount Olympus, situated near the Gulf of Themai on the Aegean Sea, alongside the twelve Olympian Greek gods and lesser deities.

The castle of the baseball gods is located in the heart of the American Elysian Fields, in the quaint village of Cooperstown. This castle comprises five interconnected buildings and is known as the National Baseball Hall of Fame and Museum.

The baseball gods include players, managers, sportscasters, writers, owners, and pioneers of the game. Only those with mystical baseball powers can pass through the pearly gates.

Very few of the 19,500 major league players have attained "god" status. As of 2024, only 247 former professional players have been inducted. Additionally, 39 executives and pioneers, 23 managers, and 20 umpires have achieved this distinguished status in baseball.

To be considered among the gods, candidates must have at least 10 years of major league experience and receive 75% of the vote from the Baseball Writers' Association of America. Some Hall-of-Famers have yet to achieve god status; their time will come only after they have passed on.

The Hall of Fame features approximately 40,000 artifacts, each with its own mystical allure. Among these relics are balls, bats, gloves, and uniforms, as well as a research center housing three million baseball-related documents.

After exploring the countryside, we made our way to the home of the gods. We purchased a ticket from Saint Peter to enter this legendary realm. While we are free to explore the exhibits, pictures, plaques, and relics, the gods themselves remain hidden, yet their presence is felt in every corner.

Upon entering this majestic structure, we joined approximately 3,000 other visitors who come each day. While I was impressed by the exhibits, I was disappointed by the minimal emphasis on the evolution of amateur and minor league baseball. A small plaque featuring Cartwright's likeness was overshadowed by tributes to lesser-known gods.

We explored numerous exhibits and memorials dedicated to baseball legends, with prominent players like Babe Ruth and Willie Mays receiving the most significant displays. The Hall seems to regard Ruth and Mays as if they were among the 12 Olympian gods.

Afterward, we visited Abner Doubleday Ballpark, located just two blocks from the Hall of Fame. A plaque on its outer wall honors Doubleday as the alleged inventor of baseball, a myth that has since been thoroughly debunked.

Later, as we enjoyed ice cream cones at a nearby deli, I said, "While the Hall of Fame hasn't designated 12 Olympian Baseball Gods, I think we should. There needs to be governance and authority over the lesser gods. Who would you choose?"

Gideon immediately replied, "Babe Ruth."

I responded, "Yes, the most famous god."

Matthew chimed in, "I would go with Willie Mays."

I said, "The greatest player ever. Scott, give me one who didn't play ball."

He thought for a while and answered, "Commissioner Kenesaw Mountain Landis."

I replied, "Very good. Great choices. I will select the other nine and share them with you tomorrow."

I had been contemplating my selections since I began

writing this book. The next morning, over breakfast, I revealed my choices and theirs. You will find all the selections detailed in this book. Here they are:

1. Alexander Joy Cartwright (1820-1892), known as the father of the game. Other notable candidates include William Wheaton, William Tucker, and Daniel "Doc" Adams.

2. Mike "King" Kelly (1857-1894), who dominated early baseball in a manner similar to Babe Ruth in the 1920s and '30s.

3. Annie Gibbons (1848-1888), a trailblazer for women in baseball, yet she has not been inducted into the Hall of Fame.

4. Shoeless Joe Jackson (1887-1951), regarded as the greatest natural hitter of all time, remains outside the Hall of Fame.

5. Babe Ruth (1895-1948), known as "The Sultan of Swat" and "The Bambino," is the most celebrated player in the history of the game.

6. Smokey Joe Williams (1886-1951), recognized as the greatest pitcher in the Negro Leagues.

7. Branch Rickey (1884-1965), who broke baseball's racial barrier by signing Jackie Robinson in 1947.

8. Judge Kenesaw Mountain Landis (1866-1944),

the first powerful commissioner dedicated to cleaning up the game.

9. Jacob Ruppert (1867-1939), the owner who launched the Yankee dynasty.

10. Willie Mays (1941-2024), widely regarded as the greatest all-around player in baseball history.

11. Mickey Mantle, celebrated as the greatest Yankee since Babe Ruth and a hero of my youth.

12. George Hancock was a pioneer of softball. Not recognized in the Hall of Fame.

I said, "Our selections include six Major League players, one Negro League player, one general manager, one owner, one pioneer of amateur baseball, one commissioner, and one pioneer of softball. Three of my picks are not in the Hall, but I'm granting them access through the back door."

Scott responded, "The 12 Olympian Gods had leaders like Zeus and Hera. Who are the baseball god leaders?"

I replied, "In our pantheon of baseball legends, your choice of Commissioner Landis is Zeus, the King of the Gods, while Annie Gibbons represents Hera, the Queen of the Gods. Their two deputies are Mickey Mantle, embodying Dionysus, the earth's benefactor and God of Wine, and Matthews' choice, Willie Mays, who symbolizes Apollo, the god of Light and artistic inspiration. Sorry, Gideon, but Ruth isn't smart enough to be a leader."

That afternoon, as we made our way back to New York to watch the Mets play the Yankees at the Mets' stadium, I looked forward to the tribute to Ebbets Field and Jackie Robinson.

As we passed by Doubleday Ballpark, I said, "When night falls and the streets are empty, the park comes alive. Some baseball gods leave the Hall and gather at Doubleday Field to play a game.

Last night, Christy Mathewson pitched against a power-hitting team led by Ted Williams and Enos Slaughter. Mathewson insisted on using a scuffed, dirty ball reminiscent of the Dead Ball Era, ultimately outmatching them as the power hitters' deep fly balls fell short of the distant fences and were caught."

Mathew said, "Your imagination is running wild, but your stories are very interesting. Tell us another one."

I replied, "This one will take a while."

Scott said, "Let's hear it."

I continued, "Once a year, the baseball gods convene for an All-Star game. Commissioner Landis selects two team owners to draft their rosters, and last year he chose Branch Rickey and Jacob Ruppert.

During their meeting, Landis tossed a bat to Rickey, and in a hand-over-hand draw, Ruppert secured the first pick.

Ruppert's first six selections were all Yankees: manager Casey Stengel; outfielders Joe DiMaggio, Mickey Mantle, and Babe Ruth; first baseman Lou Gehrig; and catcher Yogi Berra.

He then picked Ernie Banks from the Chicago Cubs to play shortstop, Nellie Fox from the Chicago White Sox for second base, and Eddie Mathews from the Atlanta Braves for third base. Mike "King" Kelly was chosen as the designated hitter.

Ruppert also selected three pitchers: Negro League star Smokey Joe Williams, and Bob Feller and Satchel Paige from the Cleveland Indians.

Rickey's first five selections were legendary Brooklyn Dodgers: manager Leo Durocher, first baseman Jackie Robinson (notably, he played first base as a rookie), catcher Roy Campanella, shortstop Pee Wee Reese, and pitcher Sandy Koufax.

He completed the infield by adding Nap Lajoie, a second baseman from the Philadelphia Athletics, and Brooks Robinson from the Baltimore Orioles at third base.

Rickey also selected two additional pitchers: Robin Roberts of the Philadelphia Phillies and Dizzy Dean of the St. Louis Cardinals.

The outfield featured Willie Mays from the Giants, Shoeless Joe Jackson from the Chicago White Sox, and Roberto Clemente from the Pirates, with Stan Musial from the St. Louis Cardinals serving as the designated hitter.

I wondered why Ted Williams from the Boston Red Sox was not chosen, speculating it might be due to his disappointing postseason performances.

Commissioner Landis appointed umpires Thomas Henry Connally (elected in 1953), Robert Calvin Hubbard (elected in 1916), and John Bertrand Conlan (elected in 1973).

As Landis, Gibbons, and Cartwright settled into their seats for the game, Landis remarked to Annie Gibbons, "I don't like Shoeless Joe playing; I banned him from participating forever."

Cartwright replied, "I didn't even want to come to this game. Baseball should have remained an amateur sport. Plus, Doubleday Ballpark is an affront to me. I deserve my place in the Hall because I am the father of the game, not because of Doubleday."

Annie Gibbons interjected, "Come on, you two, quit complaining. Landis, you're fortunate to see the best natural hitter ever. Cartwright, remember that one of your peers could have been in the Hall instead of you. Just sit back and enjoy the game."

In the press box, sportswriter Ring Lardner was pleased

to see Shoeless Joe. They had been good friends before the Black Sox scandal, and this was his chance to witness how well his old friend could still play. Lardner kept score for the game. Smokey Joe and Sandy Koufax both threw no-hit ball for the first three innings. In the fifth inning, Babe Ruth hit a home run off Roberts. Then homer from Mays off Feller in the next inning left the game tied 1-1 after six innings.

In the top of the eighth, Shoeless Joe hit a home run off Paige. In the bottom of the eighth, Mantel hit a double off Dean, which Gehrig cashed in to drive him home.

As the game entered the bottom of the ninth, the score was tied 2-2. With one out, King Kelly managed to foul off eight pitches against Dean before ultimately drawing a walk.

Kelly stole second with his famous fadeaway hook slide and quickly advanced to third. With Banks at bat, Stengel called for a squeeze play. Banks, unhappy with the decision, ignored it and struck out swinging.

Next up was Fox, and Stengel called for the squeeze play again. Fox questioned the logic of the call with two outs, believing they could easily throw to either first or home for the final out. Many of Stengel's decisions seemed puzzling, but perhaps the squeeze play would catch Durocher's team off guard.

Fox executed a perfect bunt, allowing King Kelly to sprint down the basepath and slide beneath Campanella's tag. This walk-off squeeze play clinched the game, a remarkable feat that I believe had never been accomplished before.

A celebration erupted on the field before everyone returned to the castle before dawn.

Scott remarked, "That's quite a story. You should write a fictional baseball novel. I bet it would sell."

I replied, "Yes, it would sell, but it won't be fiction. Baseball is forever—if you only believe."

Above: The Susquehanna River, near Binghamton, New York, c.1900.
Below: The Susquehanna River today, still flowing through the Promised Land.
(Courtesy Scott Wolff and Matthew Wolff)

Above: The meadow behind our rented house where I am sure baseball was once played. (Courtesy Scott Wolff and Matthew Wolff)

Right: After leaving Cooperstown, Scott, Gideon and Matthew at the Mets' ballpark watching the Mets play the Yankees. (Courtesy Scott Wolff and Matthew Wolff)

AFTERWORD

WHEN WOLFF STADIUM WAS constructed in 1994, the nearby Kelly Air Force Logistics Base was thriving, with thousands of civil service employees and airmen in its ranks. Additionally, several manufacturing plants were situated near the park. However, over the years, both the base and the manufacturing facilities have closed, causing annual game attendance to drop from 400,000 to just under 300,000.

Given these changes, we began the search for a new location for a ballpark. During my final two years as County Judge, I closely collaborated with Mayor Ron Nirenberg and Missions franchise owner D.G. Elmore to secure funding and identify a suitable site for a new stadium.

We considered placing the ballpark on the UTSA campus on the north side of San Antonio. Baseball at UTSA began in 1992, during my second year as mayor. The Roadrunners compete in NCAA Division I Baseball within the American Athletic Conference.

The university needed a new facility for its baseball team, leading us to consider constructing one that could also serve the Missions. However, working with Elmore, who resided in Indiana, proved challenging. He was hesitant to commit to his share of the stadium costs and dismissed suggestions for involving local partners.

In 2021, as Major League Baseball tightened its control

over minor leagues, it eliminated 43 minor league teams, leaving only 120—four for each of the 30 major league franchises. Including the current cut, over the years, MLB has cut a total of 344 minor league teams from its peak of 464 teams in 1949, effectively neglecting the heartland of rural America.

MLB also established new standards for player amenities. Unfortunately, our ballpark did not meet these standards for dressing rooms, dugouts, workout facilities, umpire rooms, and batting practice areas. Upgrading these facilities was projected to cost around $6 million.

Amid mounting pressure from MLB, Elmore sought to sell his franchise. Businessman Clarence Kahlig assembled investors to build a new ballpark adjacent to UTSA and developed a rendering for the facility while making an offer to purchase the franchise.

At the same time, an ownership group led by developer Randy Smith, CEO of Weston Urban, along with Bruce Hill, part-owner of the San Antonio Spurs, and former Secretary of State Hope Andrade, also submitted an offer for the franchise with plans to construct the ballpark downtown.

Ultimately, Elmore decided to sell to the Randy Smith group. On November 17, 2022, I attended the public announcement at Wolff Stadium, where plans were unveiled for a partnership with Ryan Sanders Sports and Entertainment for franchise management, with Burl Yarborough continuing to oversee the ballpark's day-to-day operations.

When Wolff Stadium was constructed, downtown San Antonio was considerably less vibrant than it is today. As County Judge and Chairman of the Commissioners Court, I spearheaded significant investments in the downtown area and collaborated closely with the city to revitalize it.

I secured funding for the restoration of San Pedro

Creek, and both the city and county provided land to UTSA for two new buildings along the creek. This development will eventually accommodate over 10,000 students attending classes downtown, alongside various projects along the creek.

The county dedicated $100 million to the Tobin Center for the Performing Arts. My wife, Tracy, serves on the board of the Alamo, which is currently undergoing a $500 million renovation. Additionally, the county contributed $25 million toward a new Alamo Museum. Nearby, several developments are emerging in Hemisfair Park, including a new hotel and apartment complexes.

Incentives from the city and county have resulted in the creation of over 10,000 housing units in the central city, making downtown an ideal location for a new ballpark.

I was excited about the prospect of a new downtown ballpark as it would complement all the investments we had made in the central city.

After serving 21 years and seven months, I opted not to run for re-election as county judge. My term ended on January 1, 2023, two months post-sale of the franchise.

On January 11, I met with my successor, Judge Peter Sakai, along with Randy Smith, Bruce Hill, and Reid Ryan. They informed me that MLB had given them three years to either upgrade the existing stadium to meet new standards or construct a new one. I encouraged them to consider locating the project along San Pedro Creek, where the county had made significant restoration investments.

Later, Randy Smith informed me that he and Graham Weston were in the process of acquiring land near the San Antonio School District administrative offices along the creek. I was pleased to learn this, as the ballpark would help activate the creek.

On June 1, 2023, I met with Hope Andrade and Bruce Hill, who shared their plan to build a park with a $34 million investment from their partnership, supplemented by funding from a tax increment district. Randy Smith and Graham Weston committed to constructing a hotel and apartments to generate additional tax revenue for the park. In the weeks that followed, Andrade and Hill updated me on their negotiations.

On August 6, I had breakfast with San Antonio Express-News Editorial Writer Josh Brodesky and Publisher Mark Medici, who requested that I write an op-ed piece.

On August 10, just four days before the city council's briefing on the ballpark, my article was published, occupying about two-thirds of the page. I concluded the piece with the statement, "Let's make the ballpark happen for the love of America's game and the betterment of our city."

On August 20, I met with eight members of COPS/METRO, a significant intercity organization. I told them I supported the new proposed park. They wanted Smith and Weston provide a $2,500 moving allowance for tenants of an aging apartment complex that is set to be replaced. I agreed with them.

In September, the City Council voted 9-2 to approve the plan, which included Smith and Weston's commitment to offer the moving allowance to tenants.

On October 8, the Commissioners Court approved the plan with a 3-1 vote and one abstention. This plan also included a commitment to construct a parking garage.

On October 15, I met with Hope and Bruce at Jim's Restaurant on Broadway. They expressed concerns about the upcoming school board vote regarding the sale of a two-acre parcel of land essential for the stadium. Ultimately, on December 16, the School Board voted 5-1 in favor of a memorandum of understanding to sell the land.

Progress on the new stadium is steady; however, completion of the new ballfield is expected to take three years. In the meantime, games will be held at Wolff Stadium.

The future of Wolff Stadium remains uncertain. There have been discussions about the Mexican Baseball League establishing a franchise in San Antonio. Founded in 1925 and based in Mexico City, this league comprises 20 teams that each play 114 games per season, featuring many former MLB players. On April 1, 2002, I attended a Mexican League game at Wolff Stadium with David Lesch and Mayor Nirenberg. We were accompanied by Cesar Cantu, owner of the Saltillo Saraperos, and Gerardo Benavides, owner of Acereros de Monclova. Both expressed interest in creating a franchise in San Antonio if the Missions were to relocate and if legal issues could be resolved.

The field could also accommodate high school and college baseball games, as well as host various other events.

I hope the city preserves the ballpark, as it holds many cherished memories from the past 30 years.

* * *

Even as this book goes to print, I couldn't let it go without mentioning what has been, for me, the most exciting time in baseball in recent memory. I am referring to the UTSA baseball team coached by Pat Hallmark.

Hallmark is a Houston native who graduated from Westbury High School, then attended Rice University where he was a star catcher for the Rice Owls. After graduating in 1995, he was drafted by the Kansas City Royals and played nine years in the minor leagues. He was an assistant coach at Rice from 2006 to 2016.

In 2019 he became the head coach of the UTSA baseball team, but 2025 has been their breakout season. Initially they were referred as "junkyard dogs" and picked to come in fourth in the American Athletic Conference. Instead, they won the regular season championship.

Out of the 64 teams that the NCAA choose to participate in regional finals only four teams were chosen that were not in the "Power Four" conferences and UTSA was one the four. Eight of 64 teams will make it to the College World Series that is held on Omaha, Nebraska.

UTSA began play in the Austin Regional Conference which was held at the University of Texas baseball stadium, Disch-Falk Field. In the first game UTSA beat Kansas State 10-2. This was their first win ever in a NCAA regional conference.

In the second game they beat the University of Texas 9-7 who was ranked number four in the nation. I stayed up to midnight watching the game. I texted Hallmark to congratulate him.

He thanked me back, "We have more to do."

And he accomplished his "more to do" by defeating the University of Texas a second time, 7-4. UTSA advanced to the super regionals to play against UCLA, the 13th ranked team in the nation. This was an amazing accomplishment.

On Tuesday afternoon, June 3, I watched the team practice as they prepared for the UCLA game to be held in Los Angeles.

I said to Hallmark, "I know you need resources to attract talent."

He replied, "No. I recruit mostly in Texas and pick talented players who UT and A&M overlook, then I develop that talent. But I do need MIL funds to retain my best players."

I said, 'We will try to raise the funds."

University sports supporters are allowed to raise funds to compensate players for their name, image and likeness. I was impressed that Hallmark only wanted funds to retain the talent he develops.

Hallmark introduced me to the players, and I had the opportunity to meet and chat with most of them.

On Saturday UTSA played a close game going into the 8th inning just 3-2 behind. UCLA then scored 3 runs in the eighth, beating UTSA 5-2. They again played a close second game, but it came unraveled in the 8th and 9th inning, with UTSA losing 7-0.

UTSA baseball has proven it can compete with the best. Hallmark just needs additional resources to continue on the road to the College World Series.

Coach Pat Hallmark (Courtesy UTSA)

INDEX

AUTHOR NELSON W. WOLFF

Nelson Wolff was a founder, together with his brother George and his dad, of Alamo Enterprises, a building materials store that established eight locations in San Antonio and South Texas. They sold the company in 1978 to a national corporation.

In 1979, he and his brothers, George and Gary, along with Ron and Don Herrmann, founded Sun Harvest Farms, a natural foods supermarket that became a nine-store chain in central and south Texas. They sold that company in 2000 to another national corporation.

Wolff has served over 33 years in public office. He served in the Texas House of Representatives and the Texas Senate in the 1970s. From 1987 to 1995 he served two terms as a City Councilman and two terms as mayor of San Antonio, the seventh largest city in the United States.

He was appointed Bexar County Judge (the top executive officer in Texas county government) in 2001 and was re-elected five times. He chose to not run for a sixth term and completed his term of office in December 2022.

A *San Antonio Express-News* editorial on December 30, 2022 said Wolff had redefined county government and that "...he retires from political life as the most consequential public official of the modern San Antonio era."

He has written eight books and co-authored one book with his wife Tracy, the founder and chairperson of the Hidalgo Foundation. Together they have six children and eight grandchildren.

Also by Nelson W. Wolff:

95 Power Principles:
Strategies for Effective Leadership in Local Government

The Mayor and the Judge:
The Inside Story of the War Against Covid

The Changing Face of San Antonio:
An Insider's View of an Emerging International City

Transforming San Antonio:
An Insider's View to the AT&T Arena, Toyota, the PGA Village
and the Riverwalk Extension

Bexar BiblioTech:
The Evolution of the Country's First All-digital Public Library

Baseball for Real Men:
Seven Spiritual Laws for Senior Players

The Heart of Bexar County
Restoration of the Bexar County Courthouse (with Tracy Wolff)

Mayor:
An Inside View of San Antonio Politics, 1981-1995

Challenge of Change:
A Struggle... A New Constitution for Texas